BASIC PHONICS FOR ADULTS
Second Edition

Phyllis Beukema
Muskegon Community College
Muskegon, Michigan

Donald Goodman
Muskegon Community College
Muskegon, Michigan

John McAlear
Lansing Community College
Lansing, Michigan

KENDALL/HUNT PUBLISHING COMPANY
4050 Westmark Drive   Dubuque, Iowa 52002

This edition has been printed directly from camera-ready copy.

Copyright © 1987, 1990 by Kendall/Hunt Publishing Company

ISBN 0-8403-5794-X

All rights reserved. No part of this publication may be reproduced, stored in a retrieval system, or transmitted, in any form or by any means, electronic, mechanical, photocopying, recording, or otherwise, without the prior written permission of the copyright owner.

Printed in the United States of America
10   9   8   7   6   5   4   3

INTRODUCTION TO THE STUDENT

Basic Phonics for Adults teaches you how to figure out words you do not recognize in your reading. You will learn to use sounds and sentence meanings to identify puzzling words. In most cases you will only need to figure out a word one time; the next time you will recognize it. You need to recognize words quickly so you can concentrate on ideas rather than on pronouncing words. If reading has been difficult for you, one reason may be that you missed learning this skill in your early school years. In this program the skills are taught at the adult level. Some of these skills you already use. By recognizing and understanding them in relation to the new skills you learn, you will use them more efficiently. You will not be doing elementary school work. This program considers that you have had adult experiences and understand complex ideas. It recognizes that you probably have above-average listening and memory skills because you often rely on these.

Cassette tapes accompany Basic Phonics for Adults. They are useful for two reasons: 1) With the text read aloud you are free to concentrate on the teachings; 2) It is important that you hear the sounds. Some words have more than one correct pronunciation. Studying and working with phonics requires careful listening. Use the tapes with each lesson and do the work as instructed. Replay any parts you need repeated; stop the tape when you need more time. You may work at your own pace.

Relax with this program; do not be afraid to make mistakes. Even good readers make errors. They often guess, skip words, or reread parts before a word makes sense. At times they read quickly; when ideas are difficult or unfamiliar, they read slowly to understand. So, be patient with yourself. Some lessons will be more difficult than others for you. You may sometimes feel frustration. When this happens talk with your instructor or tutor. With careful, thoughtful work you will recognize progress and be pleased with your improved reading ability.

Most of the work in this program is self-correcting. You will make errors. Mark your error, and next to it write the answer given in the Key. Try to understand why the answer in the Key is the better one. When you do not understand, or when you need additional practice with a particular skill, let your instructor know. Because you are an adult and working independently, your instructor counts on your asking for help when you need it.

PREFACE

Basic Phonics for Adults provides adult learners with a strategy for identifying words they do not recognize in print by teaching basic phonics skills and context clue skills. It consists of five units:

1. Nominal alphabet
2. Consonant sounds
3. Vowel sounds
4. Consonant-vowel patterns, units of sound, and other vowel sounds.
5. Combining phonics and context clues.

Presented in text-workbook form, <u>Basic Phonics for Adults</u> is accompanied by cassette tapes.

Designed by reading instructors teaching at the community college level in supervised clinic and individualized achievement lab settings, this program addresses the specific need for basic phonics instructional materials at the adult level. The presentation respects the understanding, experiences, and responsibilities of the mature student. It teaches the student what to do with unfamiliar words, thus reducing anxiety and furthering reading confidence. Reading for meaning is emphasized.

<u>Basic Phonics for Adults</u> accommodates term or semester schedules and adapts to the time constraints of individualized reading and literacy programs. It serves as supplemental work; it can be used in its entirety or in segments, as needed. Units are concise; they are appropriate for both the low-level reader with short attention span and the higher-level reader who learns more readily. The student can work independently at a separate pace, alleviating frustrations found in settings with many students and too little time for one-on-one instruction.

Skills are presented sequentially and provide an understanding of the overall phonic analysis process; this lets the mature learner understand why he is doing what he is doing. Phoneme to grapheme correspondence in regular English spelling is taught. <u>Basic Phonics for Adults</u> may very well increase a student's ability to spell. Accompanying cassette tapes permit the student to hear the sounds as he sees the word in print.

Recognizing that standardized assessment of reading skills occurs in educational settings, and that over-testing contributes to the frustrations of low-level readers, <u>Basic Phonics for Adults</u> does not pre-test for specific skills. The instructor should monitor the student at each level of the program. Quizzes provide progress checks. Self-assessment is valuable; the adult student who chooses to learn usually perceives which skills are difficult for him, which require additional practice, and which may be dealt with swiftly.

Additional exercises and suggested practices relating to independent reading for Units One through Four are included in the Appendix. Unit tests are available in the Instructor's Packet.

Introduction to the Student and Units One through Five are on tape. Students need to listen to the accompanying tape as they work in the program. After the Introduction to the Student, the tape directs students to Unit One to begin the program.

ACKNOWLEDGMENTS

Without the superhuman efforts of Janet Taylor, Secretary and Sandra Schwab, Data Processing Consultant, Muskegon Community College, this book and all its rewrites would have been impossible.

We are grateful for help and suggestions from colleagues and friends:

Allan Maar, Coordinator, Reading Instructional Services; Jackie Buher, Reading Tutor; Trudy Carpenter, Writing Instructor; Janet Hellis, Reading Instructor; Virginia Walters, Reading Instructor: Lansing Community College, Lansing, Michigan.

Elaine Brothers, Orchard View Community Education; Pam Vogas and Peg Feldt, Mona Shores Community Education: Muskegon, Michigan.

Elaine Albert, Professor Emeritus, Western Michigan University, Kalamazoo, Michigan.

Dorothy Gwynn, Retired, New Trier High School, Winnetka, Illinois.

Eunice Adams and Sue Vriesman, Muskegon-Oceana Project Literacy, Muskegon, Michigan.

Janet Ord, Kentwood Education Center, Kentwood, Michigan.

Carol Neal, Paraprofessional, Muskegon Community College, Muskegon, Michigan.

COVER DESIGN: Kristi Beukema

ILLUSTRATIONS: Ken Widing and Kristi Beukema

CONTENTS

INTRODUCTION TO THE STUDENT iii

PREFACE v

ACKNOWLEDGMENTS vii

UNIT ONE   **NOMINAL ALPHABET**
    Skill Lesson   Nominal Alphabet .... Exercise 1 3
                                                                .... Exercise 2 4
                                                               .... Exercise 3 4
    Alphabet Order .... Exercise 4 5
                                                                .... Exercise 5 5
    Review: Unit One 6
    Quiz   Nominal Alphabet .... Exercise 6 7

UNIT TWO   **PHONIC ALPHABET: CONSONANTS**

Consistent Single Consonants
    Skill Lesson   Consistent Single Consonants .... Exercise 7 11
                                                                .... Exercise 8 13
                                                                .... Exercise 9 14
    Quiz   Consistent Single Consonants .... Exercise 10 14

Inconsistent Single Consonants
    Skill Lesson   Single Consonant c .... Exercise 11 15
                                                                .... Exercise 12 15
    Skill Lesson   Single Consonant g .... Exercise 13 17
    Review   Sounds of c and g 18
    Skill Lesson   Single Consonant s .... Exercise 14 19
    Quiz   Single Consonants c g s .... Exercise 15 20
                    Single Consonants .... Exercise 16 21

    Skill Lesson   Digraphs .... Exercise 17 21
                                                                .... Exercise 18 23
                                                                .... Exercise 19 23
    Skill Lesson   Blends .... Exercise 20 24
                                                                .... Exercise 21 26
                                                                .... Exercise 22 27
    Skill Lesson   Silent Consonants .... Exercise 23 28
    Review   Unit Two 28

Quiz	Blends, Digraphs, Silent	Exercise 24	30
Application 1 Unit Two			31
Application 2 Unit Two			31

UNIT THREE — PHONIC ALPHABET: VOWELS

Skill Lesson	Long Vowels	Exercise 25	35
		Exercise 26	36
		Exercise 27	36
Quiz	Long Vowels	Exercise 28	36
Skill Lesson	Short Vowels	Exercise 29	37
		Exercise 30	37
		Exercise 31	39
		Exercise 32	39
Quiz	Short Vowels	Exercise 33	39
	Short and Long Vowels	Exercise 34	40
		Exercise 35	40
Skill Lesson	y as a Vowel	Exercise 36	41
Skill Lesson	Schwa Vowel	Exercise 37	42
		Exercise 38	45
		Exercise 39	46
Review	Unit Three		47
Quiz	Long, Short, Schwa Vowels	Exercise 40	48
Application 1 Unit Three			49
Application 2 Unit Three			50

UNIT FOUR — PHONIC ANALYSIS OF WORDS

Consonant-Vowel Patterns

Skill Lesson	Pattern VC, CVC	Exercise 41	53
		Exercise 42	54
		Exercise 43	55
Quiz	Pattern VC, CVC	Exercise 44	55
Skill Lesson	Pattern VC(e), CVC(e)	Exercise 45	55
		Exercise 46	56
		Exercise 47	57
		Exercise 48	57
Quiz	Pattern CVC(e)	Exercise 49	58
Skill Lesson	Pattern CVVC	Exercise 50	58
		Exercise 51	59
	Pattern CVVC ie words	Exercise 52	59
		Exercise 53	60

Quiz	Pattern CVVC	Exercise 54	60
Skill Lesson	Pattern CV & V Alone	Exercise 55	61
Quiz	Pattern CV & V Alone	Exercise 56	61
	Patterns	Exercise 57	62
	Patterns Pronunciation	Exercise 58	62
Review	Unit Four C-V Patterns		63
	Patterns Pronunciation	Exercise 59	64
	Patterns Pronunciation	Exercise 60	64
Application 1	Unit Four C-V Patterns		65

Units of Sound

Skill Lesson	<u>an</u> <u>en</u> <u>un</u> <u>ilt</u> <u>op</u> <u>ut</u>	Exercise 61	67
		Exercise 62	67
	<u>at</u>	Exercise 63	68
	<u>ad</u>	Exercise 64	68
	<u>atch</u>	Exercise 65	69
	<u>ight</u>	Exercise 66	69
	<u>old</u>	Exercise 67	70
Application 2	Unit Four Units of Sound		71

Additional Vowel Sounds

Skill Lesson	R-Affected Vowels	Exercise 68	72
Quiz	R-Affected Vowels	Exercise 69	73
Skill Lesson	Diphthongs <u>oi</u>-<u>oy</u>	Exercise 70	74
	Diphthongs <u>ou</u>-<u>ow</u>	Exercise 71	74
Quiz	<u>oi</u>-<u>oy</u>, <u>ou</u>-<u>ow</u>	Exercise 72	75
Skill Lesson	Diphthong ô	Exercise 73	75
Quiz	ô	Exercise 74	76
Skill Lesson	Diphthong <u>oo</u>	Exercise 75	76
Quiz	<u>oo</u>	Exercise 76	77
Review	Additional Vowel Sounds		78
Application 3	Unit Four Additional Vowel Sounds		79

Syllabication

Skill Lesson	Body of the Word	Exercise 77	81
Skill Lesson	Removing the Prefix	Exercise 78	83
Skill Lesson	Removing the Suffix	Exercise 79	84
Quiiz	Syllabication	Exercise 80	85

Application 4 Unit Four Syllabication 86
Application 5 Unit Four Syllabication 87

UNIT FIVE COMBINING PHONICS AND CONTEXT CLUES

Skill Lesson	Background Knowledge Clues	Exercise 81	91
Skill Lesson	Sentence Structure Clues: Naming Words	Exercise 82	92
Skill Lesson	Sentence Structure Clues: Action Words	Exercise 83	93
Skill Lesson	Sentence Structure Clues: Describing Words	Exercise 84	94
	Sentence Structure Clues	Exercise 85	99
Skill Lesson	Phonics and Context	Exercise 86	95
		Exercise 87	96
Skill Lesson	Paragraph Idea Clues	Exercise 88	97
Skill Lesson	Paragraphs With Titles	Exercise 89	98
Skill Lesson	Paragraphs Without Titles	Exercise 90	100
		Exercise 91	101
		Exercise 92	101
Skill Lesson	Combining Phonics and Context	Exercise 93	102
	Henry Box Brown	Exercise 94	103
	Cloth for Clothes	Exercise 95	104
	Tenting in 1910	Exercise 96	105
	Osa Johnson	Exercise 97	105
Quiz	....	Exercise 98	107

APPENDIX

Additional Exercises 113

Key 131

Bibliography 143

UNIT ONE

NOMINAL ALPHABET

STUDENT NOTES

You will find some pages marked "Student Notes." When questions come to mind as you are reading, turn to a "Student Notes" page and jot down your questions. Perhaps on page three of this book you might wonder "If w and y are sometimes vowels and sometimes consonants, how can I tell when each one is which?".

Write down your questions and ask your teacher about it later.

Also, when you are reading other assignments, perhaps questions will come into mind about new words. Write these questions and discuss them with your teacher later.

And as you read, you may encounter new, interesting words you want to remember: write them on the "Student Notes" pages. It will help you learn to read better.

UNIT ONE   NOMINAL ALPHABET

Skill Lesson   Nominal Alphabet   Exercise 1

Listed here are the twenty-six letters in the English alphabet. Name the letters and also identify which letters are the vowels. Repeat each letter after it is read, then write the letter in the blank.

Example: a (VOWEL) _a_

a (VOWEL)	____	n	____
b	____	o (VOWEL)	____
c	____	p	____
d	____	q	____
e (VOWEL)	____	r	____
f	____	s	____
g	____	t	____
h	____	u (VOWEL)	____
i (VOWEL)	____	v	____
j	____	w (SOMETIMES A VOWEL)	____
k	____	x	____
l	____	y (SOMETIMES A VOWEL)	____
m	____	z	____

When you **name** all the letters, you are using the nominal alphabet. Repeat this part of the tape until you can recite the alphabet, in the same order as above, without the tape. You may practice it in small sections, or repeat the entire alphabet over and over again.

When you name all the letters of the English alphabet, and can name each one that is a vowel letter, you then know all the vowel letters in the English language.

What about the other letters? The other letters, and sometimes w and y, are called consonant letters. By memorizing the nominal alphabet, you also know all the consonant letters in the English language. Pronounce consonant again: consonant.

Remember:

1. a, e, i, o, u, sometimes w, and sometimes y are all vowel letters.

2. b, c, d, f, g, h, j, k, l, m, n, p, q, r, s, t, v, sometimes w, x, sometimes y, and z are consonant letters.

You will learn the consonant sounds in the next unit.

Note: The English language is written from left-to-right; we read words and sentences from left-to-right. When you sound out words, you move from left-to-right.

Nominal Alphabet   Exercise 2

In the rows of letters below, underline each vowel you see. Underline w and y; they are vowels some of the time.

Example: q u h e a p y

1. f u y n o d e
2. b j a u i w o
3. t a m e o c x
4. q i s r a y o
5. v h u g e i a
6. q b y e l a u

Check your answers with the Key on page 131.

Nominal Alphabet   Exercise 3

In the words below, underline each vowel you see, including the "sometimes vowels" w and y.

Example: file   baby   flower

1. clear   2. edition   3. snow   4. crazy   5. gymnasium   6. handbook

7. feud   8. because   9. few   10. lively   11. charity   12. cowboy

Check your answers with the Key on page 131.

Alphabet Order   Exercise 4

Write each row of letters in alphabetical order, that is, the order in which they appear in the alphabet.

Example: s d j m o should be <u>d j m o s</u>

1. l h n v r _____
2. k i x p t _____
3. m j c r q _____
4. f e z s l _____
5. d y m u p _____
6. p g o v x _____

Check your answers with the Key on page 131.

Alphabet Order   Exercise 5

Write each row of words below in alphabetical order. To put words in alphabetical order, look at the first letter of each word. Then, write the words in order according to their first letter.

Example: single married divorced

Look at the first letters: s - single   m - married   d - divorced

Put the words in the same order as the first letters occur in the alphabet:

<u>**d**ivorced   **m**arried   **s**ingle</u>

1. rain clouds snow   _____
2. pencil ink marker   _____
3. nail hammer pliers   _____
4. under over next down   _____
5. king famous tyrant queen _____

Check your answers with the Key on page 131.

Unit One

REVIEW: UNIT ONE

If you need help answering the following questions, you may look back at your work in the unit exercises.

In Unit One you have learned:

1. -to name the English alphabet letters and to put them in alphabetical order.

Write the alphabet letters in alphabetical order:

__ __

Write the last names of six people you know. Be sure the names begin with different letters:

1._____ 2._____ 3._____

4._____ 5._____ 6._____

Now write the names in alphabetical order:

1._____ 2._____ 3._____

4._____ 5._____ 6._____

2. -to recognize the vowel letters.

Write the alphabet letters which are ALWAYS vowel letters: __ __ __ __ __

Write the alphabet letters which are SOMETIMES vowels and SOMETIMES consonants: __ __

3. -to recognize the consonant letters.

Write the alphabet letters which are ALWAYS consonant letters:

__ __ __ __ __ __ __ __ __ __ __ __ __ __ __ __ __ __ __ __

Write your first and last names:

_____ _____

Circle the letters which are always vowels.
Underline the letters which are always consonants.

Have your answers checked. If you have questions or want more practice with these skills before you take the Unit One quiz, see your instructor.

QUIZ   Nominal Alphabet   Exercise 6

A. Underline each vowel letter you see in the following words including the "sometimes vowels" y & w. Look carefully at the examples. Turn off the tape while you work.

Example: r<u>ai</u>n<u>i</u>ng   t<u>o</u>rn<u>a</u>d<u>o</u>   m<u>err</u><u>y</u>

1. Detroit   2. carriage   3. Sunday   4. people   5. religion

6. X-rated   7. strawberry   8. authorize 9. violence 10. clash

B. Write the following rows of letters and words in alphabetical order.

   Example:

   q f m h c   <u>c</u> <u>f</u> <u>h</u> <u>m</u> <u>q</u>

   teeth raid garage   <u>garage</u>   <u>raid</u>   <u>teeth</u>

1. w t v d r   __ __ __ __ __

2. i u f o k   __ __ __ __ __

3. Pete Don George   _____ _____ _____

4. million ten hundred _____ _____ _____

5. quick leap jump   _____ _____ _____

Have your Unit One quiz checked.

Unit One

UNIT TWO

PHONIC ALPHABET: CONSONANTS

STUDENT NOTES

UNIT TWO   PHONIC ALPHABET: CONSONANTS

CONSISTENT SINGLE CONSONANTS

Skill Lesson   Consistent Single Consonants   Exercise 7

Two Kinds of Sound

You have learned the names of the letters in the English alphabet. You have learned that the alphabet letters are either vowel letters or consonant letters. The letters stand for speech sounds. There are two kinds of sounds. One is made with all your breathing doors open. These sounds are called vowels. The second kind of sound is made by closing off one of the doors with your lips, your tongue, or your teeth. This kind of sound is called a consonant. Open sounds are vowels; closed sounds are consonants.

Sounds are Phonemes

The English alphabet has twenty-six letters but many more sounds. The sounds in language are called phonemes. One letter can make many phonemes, or sounds. For instance, you see the vowel letter a in cat, father, care, ape, ago, but the sound represented by a is different in each word. Listen carefully: cat, father, care, ape, ago. Sometimes combined letters represent a different sound, such as a and u together in taught. At times, letters are silent, such as k in knife and t in fasten. Despite these differences, in eighty percent of the common English words the consonant-vowel letters and their patterns have **consistent** sounds, that is, you can count on them to remain the same. When you know these units of sound, or phonemes, you have a tool for identifying words.

Letters are Not Phonemes; Phonemes are Not Letters

The alphabet name and the phoneme for the consonant letters are not the same. Say the word back. The name of the beginning consonant is "be"; the phoneme of the beginning consonant is the first distinct sound you hear, "b...back." In this unit you will learn the phonemes for each of the consonant letters.

Take your time on these lessons. Play the tape as often as necessary. You should be able to hear the sounds and to repeat them accurately. You will first work with the consonant phonemes that are consistent.

First: You will hear a consonant letter pronounced.
Then: A word that begins with that letter will be pronounced. REPEAT THIS WORD SOFTLY. Then, circle the consonant letter at the beginning of that word.
Next: A second word will be pronounced. REPEAT THIS WORD SOFTLY. Then, write the beginning consonant letter in the blank space.

Name of Consonant Letter	Example Word for Consonant Phoneme	
Example: b	(b)ike	b_ack
1. b	book	_eer
2. d	down	_ark
3. f	fun	_ence
4. h	hit	_and
5. j	jog	_et
6. k	kite	_ick
7. l	little	_arge
8. m	money	_ean
9. n	note	_inth
10. p	put	_est
11. q is almost always written with a u: qu	quiz	_uick
12. r	road	_anch
13. t	two	_able
14. v	vote	_est
15. w	wide	_atch
16. x	sex	e_tra
17. y	yes	_ard
18. z	zigzag	_ero

Check your answers with the Key on page 131.

Consistent Single Consonants   Exercise 8

In the list below look at the consonant in the first column. That same consonant could be found in the beginning or the middle or the end of a word. Read the consonant letter and as each word is pronounced listen for that sound. Then underline the letter in the word.

		Beginning	Middle	End
Example:	b	Boston	la<u>b</u>or	cu<u>b</u>
1.	b	but	about	crib
2.	d	dip	today	bread
3.	f	first	after	half
4.	h	hum	ahead	-
5.	j	jump	injure	-
6.	k	kind	sunken	drink
7.	l	look	believe	all
8.	m	man	amaze	from
9.	n	not	funny	when
10.	p	picture	upon	help
11.	q(qu)	quart	acquaint	-
12.	r	red	work	for
13.	t	top	little	flight
14.	v	very	even	leave
15.	w	with	always	-
16.	x	x-ray	text	fix
17.	y	you	beyond	-
18.	z	zero	razor	buzz

Check your answers with the Key on page 131.

Unit Two

Consistent Single Consonants   Exercise 9

As each word is pronounced listen for the beginning consonant sound. Write the consonant letter for the sound you hear.

Example: happy _h_   lap _l_

1. ____ 2. ____ 3. ____ 4. ____ 5. ____

Write the consonant letter for the sound you hear at the end of each word.

Example: far _r_   kid _d_

6. ____ 7. ____ 8. ____ 9. ____ 10. ____

Write the consonant letter for the sound you hear in the middle of each word.

Example: letter _t_   always _w_

11. ____ 12. ____ 13. ____ 14. ____ 15. ____

Check your answers with the Key on page 131.

QUIZ   Consistent Single Consonants   Exercise 10

As each word is pronounced, listen for the beginning consonant sound. Write the consonant letter for the sound you hear.

Example: beaver _b_   parent _p_

1. ____ 2. ____ 3. ____ 4. ____ 5. ____

Write the consonant letter for the sound you hear at the end of each word.

Example: prove _v_   quart _t_

6. ____ 7. ____ 8. ____ 9. ____ 10. ____

Write the consonant letter for the sound you hear in the middle of each word:

Example: commune _m_   rename _n_

11. ____ 12. ____ 13. ____ 14. ____ 15. ____

Have your instructor check your Quiz when you complete this unit.

INCONSISTENT SINGLE CONSONANTS: c g s

Skill Lesson   Single Consonant c   Exercise 11

Most consonants are consistent. When you try to pronounce a new word you can usually count on a consonant having the same sound every time you see it. However, the c, g, and s phonemes are **inconsistent**. They are not consistent; they are changeable.

The letter c can stand for two sounds - a hard sound and a soft sound. You hear the hard c sound in car, actor, and correct. Repeat the words to yourself and listen to the hard sound. It is a guttural, or throaty, sound made in the back of the mouth near the throat; and it sounds harsh and hard.

The other c phoneme is a soft, hissing sound. You hear it in celebrate, cylinder, and cell. Repeat these words and listen to the soft c sound.

As the words below are pronounced, listen to the c sounds. Write an H over each c having the hard sound; write an S over each one having the soft sound. Some words have two c sounds.

Example: crate (H)   cygnet (S)   bicycle (S H)

1. certain   2. coat   3. ancestor   4. occasional   5. Pacific

6. succeed   7. cigar   8. voice   9. vocal   10. coincide

11. Arctic   12. cynical

Check your answers with the Key on page 132.

Single Consonant c   Exercise 12

Soft c Sound

The following words have the soft c sound. As each word is pronounced, repeat it to yourself, listen to the soft c sound and look carefully at the underlined letters:.

           center   city   cyst
           dance   cigar   cycle
           ceiling   cider   icy

Look carefully at the vowel which follows each c:

Unit Two   15

center	city	cyst
dance	cigar	bicycle
ceiling	cider	icy

Do you notice that c is followed by an e, i, or y?

WE CAN SAY THAT c FOLLOWED BY e, i, OR y USUALLY HAS THE SOFT SOUND.

Write five words which have a soft c sound. If you cannot think of five words, look for them in your reading.

_____   _____   _____   _____   _____

Hard c Sound

The following words have the hard c sound. As each word in a list is pronounced, repeat the word to yourself, listen to the hard c, sound and look carefully at the underlined letters.

can	copy	customer	creep
cards	college	acute	actor
decay	second	curb	climb

Look carefully at the vowel or other letter, which follows each c:

can	copy	customer	creep
cards	college	acute	actor
decay	second	curb	climb

Do you notice that c is followed by an a, o, u, or a consonant?

WE CAN SAY THAT c FOLLOWED BY LETTERS OTHER THAN e, i, OR y USUALLY HAS THE HARD SOUND.

Write five words that have a hard c:

_____   _____   _____   _____   _____

Have your instructor check your work.

Skill Lesson   Single Consonant g   Exercise 13

The letter g can stand for two sounds: hard or soft. You hear the hard, guttural sound in <u>guess</u>, <u>guard</u>, <u>big</u>. The soft sound is the same as the <u>J</u> phoneme; listen for it in <u>gentle</u>, <u>gin</u>, and <u>image</u>.

As the words below are pronounced, listen for the g sound. Write H over the g having the hard sound; write S over the g having the soft sound.

Example: *H* gold   *S* page   *H S* gadget

1. gag   2. village   3. huge   4. grasslands   5. message

6. genealogy   7. pigeon   8. signature   9. regard   10. voyage

11. agree   12. genes   13. ugly   14. paragraph   15. vegetable

Check your answers with the Key on page 132.

When you are pronouncing a word with a letter g, it may help you to remember this:
(a) Usually the letter g has the hard sound, as in <u>gave</u> and <u>bag.</u>

got   jog
gun   mug
gas   wag

(b) Frequently when g is followed by e, i or y it has the soft sound, as in <u>germ</u> and <u>rage</u>
gin   ginger   page   gym   gypsy

(c) There are exceptions. When one sound does not work, then try the other sound.

Note: If we want a final g to have a soft, "j" sound, we will add an e after it:
sag - sage
rag - rage
hug - huge
Or, we can put a d in front of the g and an e behind it:
leg - ledge
bag - badge
log - lodge

Notice that the e does two things: it changes the sound of the g and it changes the sound of the vowel as well.

Unit Two

Almost any word in English which ends in c will end with the hard, "k" sound:
   critic   logic   magic   comic

And, almost any word which ends in g will end with the hard, "g" sound:
   fog   rag   pig   zig-zag   sag   hug

If we want to make a final c into a soft, "c" sound, we will add an e:
   mice   lace   farce   truce

Learning Hint: When we read and work with new ideas, we remember them better if we stop now and then and ask, "What have I just learned?" Answer yourself in your own words. If necessary, go back over the lesson. Picture in your mind which idea came first and which ideas followed from that one. You may want to use the Student Notes pages to write down your ideas.

REVIEW: SOUNDS OF c AND g:

1. **Alphabet letters stand for speech sounds.**

2. **Most consonant letters in a word are consistent:** you know what sounds to give to them. These are: b, d, f, h, j, k, l, m, n, p, q(qu), r, t, v, x, z, and y, and w when consonants. However, some consonant letters are not consistent.

3. **C usually has its SOFT sound when followed by e, i, or y.**
   Which one of these unusual words probably has a SOFT c sound? Put a check mark by your answer:

           comate   _____
           carconate _____
           cistern   _____
           culotte   _____

   Now, you write an example of a soft c word _____.

   C usually has its HARD sound when followed by a, o, u, or a consonant.

   Which one of these words probably has a HARD c sound? Put a check mark by your answer:

           cymbal   _____
           curator   _____
           civil   _____
           cinnamon _____

Now, you write an example of a hard c word _____.

4. **G usually has its HARD sound when followed by a, o, u, or a consonant.**
   Which one of these words probably has a hard g sound?

   giraffe   _____
   gangster   _____
   general   _____
   gypsy   _____

   G frequently has its SOFT sound when followed by e, i, or y.
   Which one of these words probably has a soft g sound?

   garbage   _____
   governor   _____
   gymnasium   _____
   guilty   _____

   When one sound does not work, try the other sound.

Have your instructor check your work. Ask if you want more practice with c or g sounds.

Skill Lesson   Single Consonant s   Exercise 14

The letter s may represent the
   s sound as in sin (s)
   s sound as in permission (sh)
   s sound as in his (z)
   s sound as in treasure (zh)
As the words below are pronounced, listen to the s phonemes.
   Write S   over the s if it sounds as in sin.
   Write SH   over the s if it sounds as in mission.
   Write Z   over the s if it sounds as in his.
   Write ZH   over the s if it sounds as in treasure.

   Examples: in&overset{S}{s}ane   pha&overset{Z}{s}e   pen&overset{SH}{s}ion   mea&overset{ZH}{s}ure

1. lose   2. takes   3. insurance   4. tension   5. purse

6. leisure   7. sisters   8. thousands   9. Texas

10. suppose 11. intrusion 12. commission

   Check your answers with the Key on page 132.

Unit Two

Note: Do you notice in the above exercise that words ending in <u>sion</u> may sound like:
"shun" as in pension
or
"zhun" as in division

When you see -sion at the end of a word, first try the "shun" sound, as in
    mission   possession   confession   concussion

If the word does not make sense, then try the "zhun" sound, as in
    vision   confusion   collision   excursion

QUIZ   Single Consonants <u>c g s</u>   Exercise 15

As the words below are pronounced, find each <u>c</u> and <u>g</u> in the word. Listen to their sounds. Write H over those having the hard sound; write S over those having the soft sound.

Example: gra̍ce (H S) crı̍nge (H S)

1. correction 2. genuine 3. cancer 4. describe 5. gadget

6. caged 7. circle 8. gastric 9. notice 10. ignorance

Above each letter <u>s</u>
    write S   if it sounds as in <u>sit</u>
    write Z   if it sounds as in <u>his</u>
    write SH if it sounds as in <u>mission</u>
    write ZH if it sounds as in <u>treasure</u>

Example: saw(S) busy(Z) leisure(ZH) mission(SH)

11. praises   12. Soviets   13. universities   14. television

15. refuses   16. aggression   17. Asians   18. bipartisan

19. expansion   20. lesions

    Have your Quiz checked after you complete this unit.

Single Consonants   Exercise 16

Listen carefully for the consonant phonemes as the following words are pronounced. Write the alphabet letter for the sound you hear at the beginning of these words:

Example: Dart the beginning sound in dart is "d"
Write the letter d in the blank: _d_

1. ____   2. ____   3. ____   4. ____   5. ____

6. ____   7. ____   8. ____   9. ____   10. ____

11. ____   12. ____   13. ____

Listen and write the letter for the sound you hear in the middle of these words:

Example: hiker The middle phoneme in the word hiker is "k".
Write the letter k in the blank: _k_

14. ____   15. ____   16. ____   17. ____   18. ____   19. ____

Write the alphabet letter for the phoneme you hear at the end of these words.

Example: snap The phoneme at the end of snap is "p".
Write the letter p: _p_

20. ____   21. ____   22. ____   23. ____   24. ____   25. ____

Check your answers with the Key on page 132.

If you have questions or want more practice with the single consonant sounds, see your Instructor. Otherwise, continue with your work.

Skill Lesson   Digraphs   Exercise 17

The consonant phonemes you have learned are for single consonant letters. Sometimes two consonant letters written together will have one sound. These are called consonant digraphs: ch gh ph sh th wh.

Look at the beginning of the word photo; you see p and h written together Pronounce photo and listen to the beginning sound. Your hear "f" not "p" or "h". You hear one sound that is different than either the p or h phoneme. Underline the digraph

Unit Two

in each following word: chair photo ship this when
Listen to each digraph sound: <u>ch</u>air <u>ph</u>oto <u>sh</u>ip <u>th</u>is <u>wh</u>en

Digraphs do not always appear at the beginning of words. <u>Photograph</u> has a <u>ph</u> at the beginning and at the end. <u>Brushes</u> has an <u>sh</u> in the middle.

Digraphs sounds are **not consistent**; some digraphs have a different sound in different words. Listen for them in the following exercise.

Read the consonant digraph letters in the first column. Three words will be pronounced. Listen to the sound of the digraph you see. Repeat the word softly and underline the digraph.

	<u>Beginning</u>	<u>Middle</u>	<u>End</u>
Example: ch	<u>ch</u>eese	dis<u>ch</u>arge	clut<u>ch</u>
1. <u>ch</u>	chase	exchange	such
2. <u>ch</u> as a <u>k</u> sound	chorus	hypochondriac	triptych
3. <u>ch</u> as an <u>sh</u> sound	chef	machine	mustache
4. <u>gh</u> as an <u>f</u> sound	-----	laughing	enough
5. <u>ph</u> as an <u>f</u> sound	physical	telephone	Joseph
6. <u>sh</u>	should	brushes	wash
7. <u>th</u> may have a "soft" sound as in:	this	father	lathe
8. <u>th</u> may have a "hard" sound as in:	think	anthem	fifth
9. <u>wh</u> usually has an <u>hw</u> sound	what	awhile	-----

Check your answers with the Key on page 132.

Digraphs   Exercise 18

Listen to each of these words. Pronounce the words to yourself. Underline the digraph, or digraphs, you see and hear in each word.

Example: fi<u>sh</u>   dit<u>ch</u>

1. that　　　2. ship　　　3. chop　　　4. rough　　　5. both

6. chiffon　　7. church　　8. this　　　9. with　　　10. pharmacy

11. cough　　12. wish　　13. whale　　14. Chicago　　15. which

Check your answers with the Key on page 133.

Watch for digraph letters and sounds as you read and write familiar words. You will soon recognize them also in words you do not know.

Digraphs   Exercise 19

Each digraph below is followed by three words having the same digraph sound. Write the digraphs in the blanks. One of the words will then be pronounced. Circle that word. Stop the tape player whenever you need more time.

Example: <u>ch</u> as in <u>ch</u>ain   (<u>ch</u>arge)   cat<u>ch</u>er   whi<u>ch</u>

1. <u>ch</u> as in <u>ch</u>at:　　___ocolate　musta___e　　pin___

2. <u>ch</u> as in <u>ch</u>ef:　　___aise　　___ampagne　microfi___e

3. <u>ch</u> as in <u>ch</u>oir:　　___ord　　ar___itect　　heada___e

4. <u>gh</u> as in lau<u>gh</u>:　cou___　　rou___ly　　enou___

5. <u>ph</u> as in <u>ph</u>oto:　___onics　dol___in　　digra___

6. <u>sh</u> as in <u>sh</u>eep:　___ame　　fi___ing　　ambu___

7. <u>th</u> as in <u>th</u>is:　　___em　　bro___er　　brea___e

8. <u>th</u> as in <u>th</u>ink:　___in　　me___od　　streng___

9. <u>wh</u> as in <u>wh</u>en:　___ip　　___eeze　　___am

Check your answers with the Key on page 133.

Unit Two　　　　　　　　　　　　　　　　　　　　　　　　　　　　　　　23

Skill Lesson   Blends   Exercise 20

Consonant blends are two or more consonants written and pronounced together, but unlike digraphs each letter still has its own distinctive sound. Look at the word <u>drink</u>. Consonants <u>d</u> <u>r</u> and <u>n</u> <u>k</u> are written together. Pronounce the word. Listen carefully to the <u>dr</u> and <u>nk</u> sounds. They blend, yet, you hear the sound of each letter. Read and sound from left-to-right.

   Example: <u>blend</u>   You hear "bl" at the beginning of the word.
       Write <u>bl</u>: *bl*
      You also hear "nd" at the end of the word.
       Write <u>nd</u>: *nd*

In this exercise, listen to each word. Repeat it to yourself. In the blanks write the blend you hear.

Common Consonant Blends Occurring at the Beginning of Words

<u>Alphabet letters</u>   <u>Example words</u>

  bl   black ____   blight ____

  br   bring ____   bridge ____

  cl   class ____   climb ____

  cr   cross ____   crime ____

Listen carefully as the following words are pronounced. Write the consonant blend you hear at the beginning of the word.

 1. ___ow 2. ___ean 3. ___unch 4. ___own

Listen to and repeat the word. In the blank write the blend you hear.

<u>Alphabet letters</u>   <u>Example words</u>

  dr   drew ____   drink ____

  dw   dwell ____   dwarf ____

  fl   fly ____   flag ____

  fr   from ____   freedom ____

  gl   glad ____   glass ____

Listen carefully as the following words are pronounced. Write the consonant blend you hear at the beginning of the word.

 1. ___ower 2. ___og 3. ___indle 4. ___ove 5. ___ow

Listen and repeat. In the blank write the blend you hear.

Alphabet letters   Example words

gr   green ____   grim ____

pl   please ____   plant ____

sc   scare ____   scanty ____

scr   scream ____   scratch ____

Listen carefully as the following words are pronounced. Write the consonant blend you hear at the beginning of the word.
1. ___ay   2. ___owl   3. ___ass   4. ___ape

Check your answers with the Key on page 133.

Listen and repeat. In the blank write the blend you hear.

sk   skin ____   skate ____

sl   slow ____   sliver ____

sm   smile ____   small ____

sn   snail ____   sneeze ____

Listen carefully as the following words are pronounced. Write the consonant blend you hear at the beginning of the word.
1. ___i   2. ___eeve   3. ___ore   4. ___ooth

Listen and repeat. In the blank write the blend you hear.

sp   space ____   speed ____

spl   splendid ____ splash ____

spr   spring ____   spray ____

sq   squeeze ____ squirm ____

st   stand ____   store ____

Unit Two

Listen carefully as the following words are pronounced. Write the consonant blend you hear at the beginning of the word.
    1. ___it   2. ___uirrel   3. ___age   4. ___anish   5. ___ead

---

Listen and repeat. In the blank write the blend you hear.

str	street ___	straight ___
sw	swim ___	sweat ___
tr	trick ___	train ___
tw	twin ___	twinkle ___

Listen carefully as the following words are pronounced. Write the consonant blend you hear at the beginning of the word.
    1. ___elve   2. ___ay   3. ___ange   4. ___avel
    Check your answers with the Key on pages 133-134.

Skill Lesson   Blends   Exercise 21

Common Consonant Blends Occurring at the End of Words

A blend may be found at the end of a word. Listen carefully to the blend in each word below. Write it in the blank.

Example: st   first *st* blast *st*

Alphabet letters	Example Words	
rb	absorb ___	Barb ___
ld	old ___	child ___
lf	golf ___	self ___
rf	scarf ___	surf ___
lv	solve ___	valves ___

Listen carefully then write the consonant blend you hear.
  1. we___ 2. gu___ 3. wha___ 4. de___e 5. ga___

Repeat the words as they are pronounced. Write the blend you see and hear.
<u>Alphabet letters</u>   <u>Example words</u>

    lm   film ____   helm ____

    lp   help ____   gulp ____

    mp   jump ____   camp ____

    rk   mark ____   jerk ____

Listen carefully then write the consonant blend you hear.
  1. slu___   2. qui___   3. ke___   4. rea___

Repeat the words as they are pronounced. Write the blend you see and hear.

    rn   burn ____   corn ____

    rt   mart ____   hurt ____

    rl   curl ____   snarl ____

    rm   firm ____   charm____

Listen carefully then write the consonant blend you hear.
  1. sta___   2. sto___   3. lea___   4. unfu___

        Check answers with the Key on page 134.

Skill Lesson   Blends   Exercise 22

Look at each of these words. Listen as they are pronounced. Repeat them to yourself.
Underline the blends you see and hear.

              Example: <u>cr</u>ow bo<u>ld</u> <u>s</u>no<u>rt</u>

price	sneak	blank	drive	clown	frame
chart	square	bark	twirl	spleen	form
bright	creek	glow	scold	shelf	plastic

        Check your answers with the Key on page 134.

Unit Two

Skill Lesson   Silent Consonants   Exercise 23

Some consonants are silent. Listen as the following words are pronounced. Cross out the silent consonant in each word.

Example: kh̸aki   coul̸d

b̲	debt	doubt	comb
g̲	gnat	sign	foreign
h̲	honest	hour	honor
k̲	knot	knife	knowledge
l̲	chalk	talk	would
n̲	hymn	column	solemn
p̲	pneumonia	psalm	psychology
t̲	watch	fasten	mortgage

Check your answers with the Key on page 134.

Note: There are many silent consonants in English; watch especially for these combinations **at the beginning of words**:

   gn (silent g)   kn (silent k)   pn (silent p)   ps (silent p)

REVIEW: UNIT TWO

To answer the following questions you may look back at your work in the previous exercises.

In Unit Two you have learned:

1. -that most of the single consonants have only one sound.

2. -that c̲ and g̲ may have a soft or hard sound.

   Write example words for each:

   Soft c̲ _____   Hard c̲ _____   Soft g̲ _____   Hard g̲ _____

   -that c̲ and g̲ usually have their soft sound when they are followed by__, __,or__.

28   Unit Two

3. -that s may have the "s", "z", "sh", or "zh" sound.

   Write an example word for each:

   s _____ z _____ sh _____ zh _____

4. -that consonant digraphs are two consonants written together that have one sound. They are: ch gh ph sh th wh.

   ch may sound "sh" as in _____, "k" as in _____, or as in _____.

   th may sound as in _____ or _____.

   gh may sound as in _____, ph as in _____,

   and sh as in _____.

5. -that consonant blends are two or three consonant letters written together and each consonant sound is heard.

   Write ten words having consonant blends. Circle the blends:

   1._____ 2._____ 3._____ 4._____ 5._____

   6._____ 7._____ 8._____ 9._____ 10._____

6. -that sometimes a consonant is written but not pronounced.

   Write three words that have a silent consonant. Circle the silent consonants:

   1_____ 2._____ 3._____.

   Have your instructor check your work.

Unit Two

QUIZ   Blends, Digraphs, Silent Consonants   Exercise 24

Listen as the words below are pronounced. Look carefully at the consonant letters in each word. In the blanks following a word, write each blend, digraph, or silent consonant that you see. The first four are examples.

Word	blends	digraphs	silent
father	____	*th*	____
hymn	____	____	*n*
tribe	*tr*	____	____
photograph	*gr*	*ph, ph*	____
1. stream	____	____	____
2. listen	____	____	____
3. could	____	____	____
4. blame	____	____	____
5. choral	____	____	____
6. rather	____	____	____
7. phenomenon	____	____	____
8. knees	____	____	____
9. march	____	____	____
10. psychiatric	____	____	____

Have your quiz checked when you complete this unit.

The last two exercises in this unit are Application exercises. There are similar exercises at the end of other units. In Application exercises you will apply, or use, your new learnings as you read other materials. The exercises will be read to you. Listen carefully and understand the directions. Complete the exercises later at home, or during study time at school. If you have questions, ask your instructor.

APPLICATION 1: UNIT TWO.

Look in magazines, books, newspapers, or other assignments for the words in this exercise.

Find words having the digraphs ch, sh, and wh. Write five of them below:

1. _____ 2. _____ 3. _____ 4. _____ 5. _____

Find words having the digraphs ph, th, and gh. Write five of them below:

1. _____ 2. _____ 3. _____ 4. _____ 5. _____

Find words having the blends bl, br, or pl. Write five of them below:

1. _____ 2. _____ 3. _____ 4. _____ 5. _____

Look for words having the blends sp, spl, and sm. Write five of them below:

1. _____ 2. _____ 3. _____ 4. _____ 5. _____

Look for words having the blends sw, tr, ld. Write five of them below:

1. _____ 2. _____ 3. _____ 4 _____ 5. _____ .

Have your instructor check your work.

APPLICATION 2: UNIT TWO.

How do we use the consonant phonemes to identify words? Try this when you are reading an assignment from one of your other books. Underline the words that you cannot pronounce. After you finish your reading, write ten of these words below. Include the page number on which you read the word.

Page   Word

_____   1. _____

_____   2. _____

_____   3. _____

_____   4. _____

Unit Two

_____ 5. _____

_____ 6. _____

_____ 7. _____

_____ 8. _____

_____ 9. _____

_____ 10. _____

Try to pronounce each word this way:

Underline the consonants in the word.

    Example: p<u>e</u>d<u>a</u>l

Next to the word write the consonants, leaving a gap for each vowel:

    Example: p<u>e</u>d<u>a</u>l   p__d__l

From left-to-right sound only the consonants.
Write in the vowels where they belong and try again to pronounce the word:

    Example: p<u>e</u>d<u>a</u>l

Does it sound like a word you know?
Reread the sentence in which you underlined the word.
Does that word make sense in the sentence?

Do this with each of the other words in the list. Do the best you can. If you cannot pronounce all of the words, do not worry. Go over your work with your instructor.

UNIT THREE

PHONIC ALPHABET: VOWELS

STUDENT NOTES

UNIT THREE   PHONIC ALPHABET: VOWELS

Skill Lesson   Long Vowels   Exercise 25

In Unit One you learned the names of the alphabet letters. In Unit Two you learned the phonemes, or sounds, of the consonant letters. In this unit you will learn some phonemes, or sounds, of vowel letters.

Hearing the difference between the vowel phonemes is called vowel discrimination. This is more difficult than discriminating, or separating, the consonant sounds. You may need to replay segments of this unit to hear the sounds accurately. Many students find that certain vowel sounds are more difficult than others. Let your instructor know if you want additional help or more practice exercises for a particular lesson.

In this unit you will learn three vowel sounds: long, short, and schwa. The long vowel sounds may be the easiest to learn. The long vowel sound is the same sound you hear when you say the letter name:

The long sound for the vowel letter a is the "a" you hear in raid.

The long sound for the vowel letter e is the "e" you hear in read.

The long sound for the vowel letter i is the "i" you hear in ride.

The long sound for the vowel letter o is the "o" you hear in rode.

The long sound for the vowel letter u is the "u" you hear in rude.

In the exercise below read the vowel letter in the first column. Listen to its long sound in the example words. As each word is pronounced, repeat it to yourself. In the first two words underline the vowel letter having the long sound. In the last word, write the vowel letter in the blank.

Vowel Letter	Example Word of Long Vowel Sound		
Example: a	lane	nail	t_a_pe
a	make	main	r__ce
e	neat	she	r__al
i	kite	pie	l__me
o	rode	boat	sc__ld

Unit Three   35

u   mule   fuel   __nite
Check your answers with the Key.

Long Vowels   Exercise 26

As the following words are pronounced, listen for the long vowel sounds. Mark each long vowel you hear with this mark: − . It is called a macron. Some words have two long vowels.

Example: pāne   clēan   sīlō

1. go 2. white 3. rain 4. make 5. those 6. find 7. came 8. cold 9. poke 10. like

11. union 12. grease 13. please 14. remain 15. kind 16. huge 17. relay 18. stereo
Check your answers with the Key.

Long Vowels   Exercise 27

As the following words are pronounced, listen for the long vowel sound in each. Decide which vowel you hear, and write that letter in the blank.
Example: s_le   The long vowel sound you hear is "a".
Write a in the blank: s _a_ le

t_me   t _i_ me

1. m___ 2. c___de 3. s___ne 4. s___ld 5. f___el 6. pr___view 7. m___le

8. p___in 9. gr___cery 10. s___ght 11. k___nd 12. r___m___in 13. m___an

14. p___per 15. pot___t___ 16. subscr___be 17. evalu___te 18. st___tion
Check your answers with the Key.

QUIZ   Long Vowels   Exercise 28

In the exercise below listen to the vowel sound underlined in the first word. From the other words on the line underline two words which have the same vowel sound.
Example: fake: apple ache claim dark sandy

1. fake: waist fat break war Alice

36   Unit Three

2. p_e_ople: dream   let   exercise   eager   pepper

3. b_i_cycle: bitter   climb   violent   filling   injury

4. p_o_ke: one   honest   pocket   sold   tomorrow

5. ch_u_te: punk   untie   evaluate   clutter   useful

Have your quiz checked when you complete this Unit.

Skill Lesson   Short Vowels   Exercise 29

The short vowel sounds are more difficult to discriminate. Replay this part of the tape as many times as you need to be certain you know the sounds.

Listen to the following examples of words having short vowel sounds. In the first three words underline the vowel letter having the short vowel sound. In the last word write the vowel letter in the blank.

<u>Vowel Letter</u>   <u>Example Words of Short Vowel Sounds</u>

Example	a	ran	jab	Brad	r_a_mp
	a	hat	pan	man	m__tch
	e	bet	well	men	r__nt
	i	sit	if	in	p__ck
	o	top	job	hot	f__nd
	u	but	muss	sun	j__st

Check your answers with the Key.

Short Vowels   Memory Aid   Exercise 30

You may find a **memory aid** helpful for remembering the short vowel sounds. Have you used the sentence "In fourteen hundred ninety-two Columbus sailed the ocean blue" to help you remember that Columbus supposedly discovered America in 1492? If you did, you were using a memory aid. To remember the short vowel sounds, try a memory aid.

Unit Three

Examples: bad   men   in   hot   sun
           a   e   i   o   u

           mad   hen   in   hot   tub
           a   e   i   o   u

A silly phrase or sentence helps you recall the short sounds of each vowel: "a" "e" "i" "o" "u". Your own ideas may work better for you. On the line below, write a memory aid sentence of your own to help you remember the short vowel sounds.

_____

Have your instructor check your word selections to be certain they are accurate examples of the sounds.

Short Vowels   Exercise 31

As each of the following words is pronounced, listen for the short vowel sound. Mark each short vowel with this mark: ˘   It is called a breve.

Examples: păn   sĭn   ŭs

1. in   2. pat   3. thumb   4. jump   5. spot   6. uncle   7. wreck   8. skill

9. wax   10. think   11. hell   12. bus   13. Smith   14. match   15. phlox

Check your answers with the Key.

Short Vowels   Exercise 32

As the following words are pronounced, listen for the short vowel sounds. Decide which vowel sound you hear and write that letter in the blank.

Example: Listen to p__ck.
The short vowel sound you hear is "i", the short sound for the letter i.
Write i in the blank: p_ĭ_ck

1. p__t   2. __nder   3. h__mble   4. k__tten   5. r__t   6. s__ster   7. p__cket

8. r__cord   9. c__t   10. g__tting   11. w__nter   12. str__nded   13. s__t   14. p__cket

15. r__ckless   16. s__ccess   17. p__t   18. c__ntract   19. r__cket   20. m__del

Check your answers with the Key.

QUIZ   Short Vowels   Exercise 33

As the first word in each line below is pronounced, listen to the sound of the underlined vowel. From the other words on the line, underline two words which have that same vowel sound.

Example: c<u>u</u>p: cute   s<u>u</u>ction   fuel   although   <u>u</u>pper

1.   <u>a</u>nd: laugh   already   wave   rabbit   aviation

2.   <u>e</u>lk: jet   lean   eight   meteor   belly

3.   sl<u>i</u>p: blind   bitter   visor   bike   pickle

Unit Three   39

4. f<u>o</u>nd: cover robin soap opera sparrow

5. c<u>u</u>p: success cupid educator lubricate utter

Have your quiz checked when you complete this unit.

Short and Long Vowels   Exercise 34

As the following words are pronounced, listen for the vowel sound in each. Mark the vowel having the short sound with the breve (˘); mark the vowel having the long sound with the macron (−). Some vowels are silent and will not be marked at all.

Examples: slĭm   cūbe   dŏt

1. bat 2. send 3. boat 4. huge 5. mop 6. cave 7. lid 8. hold

9. seal 10. robe 11. tub 12. child 13. can 14. pale 15. use 16. let

17. fin 18. load 19. not 20. read 21. line 22. fuse 23. hope 24. ape

Check your answers with the Key.

Skill Lesson   Short and Long Vowels   Exercise 35

A study guide can help you discriminate the vowel sounds. On a sheet of paper, or a 3" x 5" card, copy the chart below. It gives examples of each of the long and short vowel sounds. Turn off the tape while you work.

Vowel Letter	**Vowel Sounds**	
	<u>Long</u>	<u>Short</u>
a	made	mad
e	mean	men
i	ride	rid
o	hope	hop
u	use	us

As you work an exercise, use the chart this way: If you are deciding whether dabble has the long a or short a sound, compare it with the a sound in the examples. Listen as you say

        dabble: made
        dabble: mad

In which combination are the two sounds alike? It is in "dabble: mad". The a in dabble has its short sound. As you compare sounds, they become familiar to you, and soon you can identify them without referring to the chart.

Place your study guide beside your work and compare sounds as you do the following exercise. 1) Listen as each word is pronounced; 2) Pronounce each word to yourself and listen to the vowel sound. If you are not sure if the vowel has its short or long sound, compare its sound with the sound of the vowel on the chart. 3) Mark the short vowel sounds with the breve (˘) and the long vowel sounds with the macron (–).

Turn off the tape if you need more time to work.
        Examples: slim cube dot

1. hate 2. clock 3. June 4. oats 5. pen 6. chat 7. wild 8. rub 9. close

10. real 11. fold 12. kid 13. loaf 14. pin 15. pet 16. cute 17. male 18. pan
        Check your answers with the Key.

Skill Lesson   Y as a Vowel   Exercise 36

Y is a vowel when it has a vowel sound. When it has a long vowel sound, it is considered a long y. When it has a short vowel sound, it is called a short y.

    Example: In the word dye: y sounds like a long i.
                      In the word Betty: y sounds like a long e.
                      In the word hymn: y sounds like a short i.

Listen as the following words are pronounced. Mark each y having a long sound with a macron (–), and each y having the short sound with a breve (˘).

        Example: fly happy symbol

1. hurry 2. Netty 3. cycle 4. baby 5. any 6. myth 7. dying 8. Sally

9. pretty 10. system 11. my 12. symptom 13. study 14. psyche 15. dynamo
        Check your answers with the Key.

Unit Three

Note: In Unit Four you will work with w as a vowel. Y is a consonant when it has the "y" sound as in yes. W is a consonant when it has the "w" sound as in walk. When y has a vowel sound, it is a vowel. When w is part of a vowel sound, it is a vowel, as in paw, slow.

Skill Lesson   Schwa Vowel   Exercise 37

Another vowel sound is the schwa. It is the "uh" sound, almost the same sound as the short u. Any vowel may have the schwa sound. You hear it in:

>the a in aside
>
>the e in bullet
>
>the i in rancid
>
>the o in offend
>
>the u in circus
>
>the y in methyl

The schwa sound is neither short nor long. It may help you to add the schwa sound to your short vowel memory aid sentence:

Bad	men	in	the	hot	sun
a	e	i		o	u

Unit Three

Mad	hen	in	th<u>e</u>	hot	tub
a	e	i		o	u

The schwa vowel sound is more difficult to hear than short or long vowel sounds. Listen carefully to the schwa sound in the following words. The schwa vowels are highlighted.

Indi**a**n   p**o**litics   celebr**a**te   reas**o**n   milit**a**nt   for**e**st

pamphl**e**t   **a**gree   hospit**a**l   myst**e**ry   pr**o**gressi**o**n   giant

Understanding why some vowels sound "uh" rather than short or long may help you hear the sound. The reason involves syllables and accent. This is more complex than your previous work, so we will go step-by-step.

I. SYLLABLES

Many words have more than one vowel sound.
    In <u>June</u> you hear only one vowel sound: J<u>u</u>ne.
    In <u>April</u> you hear two vowel sounds: <u>A</u>pr<u>i</u>l.
    In <u>Michigan</u> you hear three vowel sounds: M<u>i</u>ch<u>iga</u>n
    <u>Continuously</u> has five vowel sounds: c<u>o</u>nt<u>i</u>n<u>uou</u>sl<u>y</u>.
Each word part in which you hear one vowel sound is called a **syllable**.

Unit Three

As each word below is pronounced, listen for the vowel sounds. Underline the vowel sounds you hear; remember, some vowels are silent. On the blank following the word, write the number of vowel sounds, or syllables, you hear in the word.

Example: g<u>o</u>t _1_   c<u>a</u>ref<u>u</u>l _2_

swimming ____   vibrate ____   technical ____   video ____   smokestack ____

kerosene ____   defensibility ____   harmonica ____   carefully ____

Check your answers with the Key.

2. ACCENT

When we speak naturally, our voices rise and fall rhythmically.
   Listen to Alaska.
   We do **not** say: <u>A</u> las ka   or   A las <u>ka</u>
   We **do** say: A <u>las</u> ka
   We give the syllable "las" more emphasis, or stress.
   This is called **accent.**

Listen to the accent on the syllable "mu" in <u>community</u>: com**mu** nit y   com **mu** nity. In the dictionary the **/** , the stress mark, is used to show which syllable, or syllables, are accented. A heavier mark indicates the strongest accent; a lighter mark shows a lighter accent. In most dictionaries the stress mark is placed <u>after</u> the syllable.

Examples: hap′py   schiz′o phren′ic   com mu′nit y

In the following words try to hear and mark the syllable that is accented.
Use the stress mark:
   Ath ens   man do lin   prof it
You were correct if you marked this way:

   Ath′ens   man do lin′   prof′it

On the syllables which are not accented, the vowel loses its short or long sound; instead it is weak and unclear. It has a soft "uh" sound; this is the **schwa** sound. You hear it on the <u>un</u>accented syllables.

Example: <u>com</u> mu <u>nit</u> y   Ath <u>ens</u>   man <u>do</u> lin   prof <u>it</u>   <u>A</u> las <u>ka</u>

Thinking of drumbeats may help you better understand the schwa sound. A drummer hits some beats softly and others harder. Our voice "beats" some word syllables harder than it does others. On the softer "beats" the vowel sound comes out only a faint "uh": this is the schwa sound.

As each of the following words is pronounced, repeat the word to yourself. Listen for the voice drops. Underline the schwa vowel, that is, the vowel having the "uh" sound in the unaccented syllable.

Example: loc<u>a</u>l   lin<u>e</u>n   <u>o</u>bserve

1. patent   2. opal   3. oppose   4. divine   5. hopeful

Note: Keep word sounds as they are usually spoken. Sounds can easily be distorted, or changed, when you repeat a word very slowly and stretch it out like a rubber band.
For example: pat ent   com mu nit y.

To hear normal speech sound, listen carefully as you repeat the word rapidly three or more times.

For example: patent, patent, patent   community, community, community

Repeat the following words rapidly as you continue underlining the schwa vowels:

6. rapid   7. chicken   8. organ   9. unless   10. melon

11. summit   12. private   13. parcel   14. fragrant   15. object

Check your answers with the Key

Discriminating the schwa sound is often difficult; do not be discouraged if you make more errors than in previous exercises. When you need to know for certain which syllables have the schwa sound, you can check the word in the dictionary. For now, practice listening for it.

Schwa Vowel   Exercise 38

The dictionary sign for the schwa sound is an upside down <u>e</u> (ə).

As you hear each word pronounced, listen for the schwa sound. Write the upside down <u>e</u> over each vowel having the schwa sound.

Group One: Each word in this group has one schwa sound. Mark it.

Example: əway   kittən

brilliant   canal   canopy   erect   broken   canary

candle   evasion   prison   comma   Duluth   family   apple

Unit Three   45

Group Two: Each word in this group has two schwa sounds. Mark them.

    Canada   maternity   convulsion convention scandalous

    subversion   converter   opossum   intelligence apostle

Group Three: Each word in this group has three schwa sounds. Mark them.

    submersible   America   authoritarian   institutionalize

This word has four schwa sounds: subordinationism. Want to try it?
                            Check your answers with the Key.

Note: The world will not come to an end just because you pronounce the sound as a short vowel instead of a schwa. In fact, you will probably be able to come close to pronouncing the word if you do that. It will just sound a little funny, but you may be close enough to recognize the word in the sentence or paragraph you are reading.

Schwa Vowel Exercise 39

Add examples of the schwa sound and the y-vowel sounds to your study guide.

Vowel Letter	Vowel Sounds		
	Long	Short	Schwa
a	made	mad	allow
e	mean	men	client
i	ride	rid	margin
o	hope	hop	lesson
u	use	us	focus
y	fly (i)	gym (i)	
	baby (e)		

Refer to your study guide as you work this exercise. As each word below is pronounced, listen carefully to the vowel sounds. Mark the long vowels −, the short vowels ᴗ, and the schwa vowels ə.

Example: āprə̄n tĭptŏp sy̆mbəl

1. awaken 2. sudden 3. prison 4. puny 5. seldom 6. frozen 7. felon 8. riot

9. ballot 10. hasten 11. punted 12. lesson 13. atom 14. hammock 15. human

Check your answers with the Key.

REVIEW: UNIT THREE

Refer to your work in the previous exercises if you need help answering the following questions.

In Unit Three you have heard three different vowel phonemes: long, short, and schwa.

1) For each of the following vowels write a word having a short vowel sound. Underline the vowels having a short sound.

   a _____

   e _____

   i _____

   o _____

   u _____

2) For each of the following vowels write a word having a long vowel sound. Underline the vowels having a long sound.

   a _____

   e _____

   i _____

   o _____

   u _____

Unit Three

3) The letter y is a vowel when it has a vowel sound. Write three words with a y having a vowel sound:

_____   _____   _____

4) A syllable is each word part that has a _____ sound. On the syllable, or syllables, which are unaccented the vowel sound is weak; it sounds like "uh".
This is the _____ sound.

Write four words having one or more schwa sounds, then circle the schwa vowels.

_____   _____   _____   _____

Discuss your work and your questions with your instructor, and determine if you need additional practice with the vowel sounds in this unit.

QUIZ   Long, Short, Schwa Vowels   Exercise 40

In each line below listen to the sound of the underlined vowel in the first word. From the other words on the line, underline the word which has that same sound.

Example: about: candy   margin   slowly   making

1. send: clean   suggest   relief   break

2. nut: cute   fluffy   ukelele   quit

3. seat: jet   concede   ripe   runner

4. mat: place   meat   happy   away

5. home: foot   promise   hopping   volt

6. flit: kite   mind   gym   dynamite

7. lane: weigh   fan   lantern   awoke

8. hop: piano   storm   open   octane

9. apart: fancy   common   hiking   Andrew

10. cute: butter   rough   cut   uniform

11. twine: swimmer   twin   sight   Christmas

48   Unit Three

12. sympt<u>o</u>m: bombshell   away   seacoast   shooting

Have your quiz checked at the end of this unit.

The schwa is the most common vowel phoneme in the English language. When you use vowel sounds to identify a word, first try the long and short sounds. If the word sounds strange, try the schwa sound.

Note: Listen carefully to the directions for the following Application exercises.

APPLICATION 1: UNIT THREE   WORDS YOU CAN PRONOUNCE

From other pages in this book find ten words that have two or more syllables, and that you **do** know how to pronounce. Write them below with the page number on which you found the word.

___ I. _____

___ 2. _____

___ 3. _____

___ 4. _____

___ 5. _____

___ 6. _____

___ 7. _____

___ 8. _____

___ 9. _____

___ 10. _____

Do this with each word:
  Pronounce the word and underline each vowel you hear.
  Listen carefully to the sound of each underlined vowel.
  Mark each vowel this way:
    ⌣   for a short sound
    –   for a long sound
    ə   for a schwa sound
    N   for a vowel sound that is not short, long, or schwa.
      Have your instructor check your work.

Unit Three

APPLICATION 2: UNIT THREE
WORDS YOU CANNOT PRONOUNCE

From your reading find three words that have two or more syllables, and that you **do not** know how to pronounce. In the first blank, write the word. Leave the next space blank. On the following two lines write the sentence in which you found the word.

1. _____   _____

   _____

   _____

2. _____   _____

   _____

   _____

3. _____   _____

   _____

   _____

Now, do this with each word:

In the space following the word, write the consonants you see in the word. Leave a gap for each vowel.

        Example: frantic   fr_nt_c

From left-to-right sound the consonants.

Write in the vowels.

Sound the consonants and the vowels:
    Try the short vowel sound or the long vowel sound.
    Does it make a familiar word?
    If not, try a schwa sound for one of the vowels.
    Reread the sentence in which you found the word.
    Can you sound a word that makes sense in the sentence?

Do this with each word. Do the best you can. If you cannot pronounce all the words, do not worry. Go over your work with your instructor.

UNIT FOUR

PHONIC ANALYSIS OF WORDS

CONSONANT-VOWEL PATTERNS

UNITS OF SOUND

ADDITIONAL VOWEL SOUNDS

SYLLABICATION

STUDENT NOTES

UNIT FOUR   PHONIC ANALYSIS OF WORDS

CONSONANT-VOWEL PATTERNS

Pattern One: VC, CVC

Skill lesson   Pattern VC, CVC   Exercise 4I

In Unit Three you worked with the long, short, and schwa vowel sounds. Later in this unit you will learn additional vowel sounds. First, there are ways to figure out when a vowel is likely to have a short or long sound. Looking at the letters around the vowel, and <u>seeing</u> how the consonants and vowels are grouped, helps you pronounce the vowel sound. These are called consonant-vowel patterns. The abbreviations and markings used in this lesson are:

v	vowel letter
c	consonant letter
⌣ (breve)	short vowel sound
− (macron)	long vowel sound
/ (slash)	silent letter

There are four common consonant-vowel (C-V) patterns:
1. Pattern VC, CVC
2. Pattern VC(e), CVC(e)
3. Pattern CVVC
4. Pattern CV & V Alone

Look at the first pattern. When you have a vowel and then a consonant, or consonants, the vowel sound will probably be short.

Examples: v̆c   ăt   ŏn   ĭs
          v̆cc   ănd
          v̆ccc ĭnch

There may be a beginning consonant in this pattern; if so, the vowel sound remains short.

Examples: cv̆c   băt
                 pŏt
                 pŏd
                 rŭg
                 bĕt

If consonants, digraphs, or consonant blends are added to either side of the vowel, the vowel continues to be short; that is, the pattern remains the same.

Examples: cv̆c   căt
          ccv̆c   scăt
          ccv̆cc scrătch

Unit Four

Listen carefully as CVC pattern words are pronounced. As each word is pronounced, repeat the word to yourself. Example: track.

Then turn off the player and do this:

1. Find the vowel and write V under it: t r a c k.
                                              V

2. Find all the consonants and write C under each one: t r a c k.
                                                         c c V c c

3. Underline the CVC pattern: t r a c k.
                                 c c v c c

4. In the word, mark the short vowel with the breve (ᵕ): t r ă c k.
                                                           c c v c c

5. Turn on the player and go to the next word.

Try the first five:

1. dish   2. stop   3. skunk   4. brand   5. tent

Check your answers with the Key. Correct your errors.

Continue with these words:

6. clot   7. scant   8. drug   9. smack   10. sled

11. drop   12. plant   13. frisk   14. thumb   15. stretch

Check your answers with the Key.

Pattern VC, CVC   Exercise 42

The following words are both VC and CVC patterns. Listen as they are pronounced. After each pronunciation, repeat the word to yourself. When all the words have been pronounced, turn off the player and do this:
1. Underline the letters that make the VC or CVC pattern in each   word.
   Examples: <u>add</u>   pl<u>ant</u>
2. Then mark the vowel with the breve (ᵕ) to indicate the short sound.
   Examples: ădd   plănt

1. list   2. add   3. film   4. slush   5. dock   6. bet   7. egg   8. dent

9. imp   10. mat   11. bomb   12. snob   13. end   14. grunt   15. twin

Check your answers with the Key.

54   Unit Four

Pattern VC, CVC   Exercise 43

This pattern is found not only in simple words. It is also found in syllables, or parts, of longer words. Listen as the following longer words are pronounced. They are divided into syllables. Underline each syllable having the VC or CVC pattern. Mark the short vowel with a breve (⌣). Do not mark every syllable, only the ones with VC or CVC pattern.

Example: <u>lĭst ĭng</u>   <u>ĕmp</u> ty

Continue:
1. mul ti ply   2. pro test   3. Ken neth   4. in val id   5. pan ic

6. ex act ly   7. in vest   8. sup ply   9. ex pect   10. in sult

Remember: When you have a vowel and then a consonant, or a consonant-vowel-consonant, the vowel sound will probably be _____.

Check your answers with the Key.

QUIZ   Pattern VC, CVC   Exercise 44

In each word below, underline each syllable having the VC or CVC pattern and the short vowel sound. Then mark the short vowel in the pattern with a breve (⌣).

Example: <u>căn nŏt</u>   <u>ĭn</u> vite   <u>ĕx</u> ceed   <u>chĭn</u>

1. dent   2. bob sled   3. in vest   4. re trench   5. slit   6. but   7. help ing

8. stretch   9. re tell   10. un fair   11. Bap tist   12. scant y

Have your instructor check your Quiz after Exercise 60.

Pattern Two: VC(e), CVC(e)

Skill Lesson Pattern   VC(e) and CVC(e)   Exercise 45

Look at another pattern: VC(e), CVC(e). When a vowel is followed by a consonant and then a final e, the first, or middle, vowel is usually long and the final e silent:

Example: v̄c(e̸) īce̸
                   āte̸
                   ūse̸

There may be a beginning consonant, or beginning consonants, in this pattern. If so, the vowel usually remains long and the final e silent:

Example: c̄vc(e̸)   glōbe̸   strīpe̸

Unit Four   55

Listen carefully as VC(e) and CVC(e) pattern words are pronounced. As each word is read, repeat the word to yourself. Turn off the player and do this:

1. Find the vowel you hear and write V under it: b i t e.
                                                    V

2. Find the final e and write e under it: b i t e.
                                             V   e

3. Find all the consonants and write C under each one: b i t e.
                                                        C V C e

4. Underline the VC(e) or CVC(e) pattern: b i t e.
                                           C V C e

5. Mark the long vowel with the macron (−) and the silent e with the slash (/): b ī t ḙ.
                                                                                 C V C e

6. Turn on the player and go to the next word.

Try the first five:
1. p h o n e   2. e k e   3. s c r a p e   4. c u b e   5. f i n e

Check your answers with the Key, then continue.

6. f a t e   7. s h i n e   8. a g e   9. r a c e   10. s t y l e

11. b o n e   12. m u l e   13. U t e   14. t h e s e   15. e v e

Check your answers with the Key.

Pattern VC(e), CVC(e)   Exercise 46

Remember, patterns of sound apply to syllables as well as words. Listen as these longer words are pronounced. They are divided into syllables. Underline the syllable having the VC(e) or CVC(e) pattern. Include the additional consonants. Mark the long vowel with a macron (−) and the silent e with a slash (/).

Example: dis grācḙ   ath lētḙ   in trūdḙ

Now do these:
1. in flate   2. dis trib ute   3. re cede   4. up grade   5. hope ful

6. oc tane   7. mis take   8. di vide   9. states man   10. time ly

Remember: When a vowel in a word or syllable is followed by a consonant and then a finel e, the vowel is usually _____ and the final e is _____.

Check your answers with the Key.

Patterns CVC and CVC(e)   Exercise 47

Change the following short vowel words to long vowel words. Do it this way:

1. Pronounce the first word: Example: mat_____

2. Write that word on the line and add an e to the end of it: mat *mate*

3. Pronounce both words: mat *mate*

4. Go to the next one.

When you have finished this exercise, check all your pronunciations with the tape. Now turn off the tape and write.

1. hat_____   2. fin_____   3. cap_____   4. not_____   5. shin_____

6. kit_____   7. rob_____   8. rid_____   9. rat_____   10. dim_____

Patterns CVC and CVC(e)   Exercise 48

The words in this exercise are "nonsense" words. That is, they are words that will not make any sense to you. They will not be words that are familiar to you. However, they all follow either the CVC pattern or the CVC(e) pattern. As you hear each word write it on the line provided.

                 Examples: et   hame   stim   lipe

Listen and write:

1._____   2._____   3._____   4._____   5. _____

6._____   7._____   8._____   9._____   10. _____

                 Check your answers with the Key.

Unit Four

QUIZ   Pattern CVC(e)   Exercise 49

In each word below, underline each syllable having the VC(e) or CVC(e) pattern. Then, mark the vowels in the pattern long (−) or silent (/).

Example: un wise̅   con fu̅se̸

1. hope   2. name sake   3. com pute   4. dic tate   5. un used   6. com bine

7. use less   8. de vote   9. com plete   10. back bone   11. name less   12. flag pole

Have your instructor check your quiz after Exercise 60, the last exercise in this unit.

Pattern Three: CVVC

Skill Lesson   Pattern CVVC   Exercise 50

When two vowels are written together, there are several possible sound patterns. The common one is that the first vowel has its long sound and the second vowel is silent. (Example: o̅a̸t). The pattern remains the same when consonants are added. (Example: bo̅a̸t   thro̅a̸t).

As the words below are pronounced, mark the long vowel with the macron (−) and cross out the silent vowel (/). Some words in each row are marked for you.

<u>ea</u> <u>ee</u> <u>ei</u> <u>ey</u> words:

me̅a̸n	heal	cheap	read	we̅e̸d	teen
meet	speak	easy	freak	cheek	sleek
either	leisure	receive	seize	donke̅y̸	kidney

<u>ai</u> <u>ay</u> words:

| bait | plain | main | pa̅y̸ | may | say |
| hay | claim | Spain | spray | tray | |

<u>oa</u> <u>oe</u> <u>ow</u> words:

| oats | moan | coal | Joan | roast | loaf | coach |
| do̅e̸ | Joe | foe | hoe | flo̅w̸ | slow | blow |

Check your answers with the Key.

Note: Watch out for the exceptions. When you pronounce an ei or ey word with the long e sound and the word does not make sense in a sentence, try a long a sound:

    eight   weight   freight   neighbor   reindeer

    hey   they   prey   obey   survey

Pattern CVVC   Exercise 51

The CVVC pattern is found in syllables as well as in simple words. The longer words below have been divided into syllables. Find the CVVC syllable in each word and underline it.   Example: toast er   <u>toast</u> er

Turn off the tape while you underline:

1. load ed   2. plead ing   3. treat ment   4. con tain er   5. ex claim

6. faint ed   7. roast er   8. pro ceed   9. be neath   10. re frain

11. ap pear   12. mean ing   13. clean est   14. McClain   15. bloat ed

Now, as each word is pronounced mark the long vowel with the macron (−) and the silent vowel with the slash (/).

    Check your work with the Key.

Pattern CVVC ie Words   Exercise 52

The CVVC pattern is not consistent; it is not always CV̄V̸C. Sometimes the first vowel is silent and the second is long: CV̸V̄C.

    Example: st/eāk   y/eōman

This commonly occurs in ie words; often the i is silent and the e is long: ch/iēf. The ie words are often difficult to spell, as well as to pronounce.

Listen to the vowel sounds in following ie words. Mark the silent vowels with a slash (/) and the long vowels with the macron (−). The first two words are marked for you.

1. f/ield   2. gr/ēve   3. thief   4. shield   5. piece   6. siege   7. yield   8. diesel

9. believe   10. achieve   11. priest   12. wiener   13. niece   14. hygiene   15. chief

Remember: When you see an ie word you may need to pronounce the e _____ and make the i _____ .

    Check your answers with the Key.

Unit Four

Note: Some <u>ie</u> words **do** conform to the CVVC pattern:
    tie   die   lie   pie   vie

Pattern CVVC ie Words Exercise 53

As the previous words are pronounced again, write each word in the blanks below:

1._____ 2._____ 3._____ 4._____ 5._____

6._____ 7._____ 8._____ 9._____ 10._____

11._____ 12._____ 13._____ 14._____ 15._____

Check your spellings with the Key.

If you misspelled a word, cross it out and rewrite it correctly. Pronounce the word as you write it.

Complete the following sentence:

When two vowels are written together in a short word or a syllable, one vowel often has the _____ sound and the other is _____. Try one pronunciation. If the word does not make sense in the sentence, try the other pronunciation.

Check your answers with the Key.

QUIZ Pattern CVVC Exercise 54

In each word below, underline each syllable having the CVVC pattern. Then, mark the vowels in the pattern long (−) or silent (/).

Example: gr<u>eat</u>   a v<u>ail</u>   <u>east</u> ern

1. bloat   2. feet   3. steam boat   4. a fraid   5. im peach   6. weav er

7. ail ment   8. leaf let   9. car load   10. black mail   11. oat meal   12. pot roast

Have your Quiz checked after Exercise 60.

Pattern Four: CV & V Alone

Skill Lesson   Pattern CV & V Alone   Exercise 55

When a vowel comes at the end of a syllable or word, that vowel often has the long sound: CV.

Examples: mē   flȳ   rō dent   ō lē ō

The number of consonants before the vowel may vary, and the vowel will remain long.

Examples: hē   shē

Sometimes a vowel alone forms a syllable, and the vowel often will have its long sound.

Examples: ā ble   ō le ō   ē go

Listen as the following words are pronounced. Underline the syllable having the CV pattern or the V alone. Repeat the word to yourself and mark each long vowel with a macron (−).

Example: lā bor   mā son   ō lē ō

1. so   2. Jel lo   3. lo cate   4. man go   5. ster e o

6. la dy   7. cu pid   8. flu   9. so lo   10. hap py

Complete this sentence: When a vowel comes at the end of a word or syllable, or when a vowel is alone in a syllable, it often has the _____ sound.

Check your answers with the Key.

QUIZ   Pattern CV & V Alone   Exercise 56

In each word below, underline the syllable having the CV pattern or the V alone. Mark each long vowel with a macron (−).

Example: rē state   tor nā dō   ē vil

1. ve to   2. jum bo   3. ba sic   4. Plu to   5. i ris   6. cra dle

7. so ber   8. bi son   9. e qual   10. re port   11. ba con   12. ac ne

Have your Quiz checked after Exercise 60.

Unit Four

Patterns   Exercise 57

This exercise includes the four patterns. Each word has a short or long vowel sound. Some may have a silent vowel. Mark the short vowels with a breve (˘), the long vowels with a macron (−), and the silent vowels with a slash (/).

Example: hēa̸l   sān̸g   Pă̆m   fly̅

Listen and mark these vowels as the words are pronounced:

1. peak	2. in cline	3. had	4. grieve	5. lay	6. grain
7. goes	8. bland	9. strike	10. piece	11. soak	12. fuse
13. chief	14. freed	15. dis may	16. pray	17. smoke	18. boast
19. why	20. bus				

Check your answers with the Key.

Patterns   Pronunciation   Exercise 58

Below are examples of the four sound patterns CVC, CVC(e), CVVC, and CV. Turn off the tape and read these pairs of words. Then turn on the tape and listen as they are repeated:

at	ate
pet	Pete
cut	cute
fin	fine
cot	coat
peck	peak

Do you SEE all the letter patterns you have been learning? Do you HEAR the difference between the short and long vowel sounds? Here is another set. Careful: These have mixed patterns. Turn off the tape and read, then listen as they are repeated:

slid	slide
seat	set
clam	claim
rap	rape
bead	bed
same	Sam

Unit Four

Here is another set of short-vowel and long-vowel words. Read and pronounce them as you did in the other exercises:

met	meat	me
go	got	goat
feed	fed	feat
mull	mule	
reed	red	read
made	mad	maid

REVIEW: UNIT FOUR   CONSONANT-VOWEL PATTERNS

Seeing how the vowel and consonant letters are grouped helps us know whether the vowel sound will be short or long. The four common groups, or patterns, are:

1. VC, CVC

When a word or syllable has one vowel and it comes before a consonant or between consonants, usually it has its _____ sound.

Give three example words which follow this pattern.

_____   _____   _____

2. CVC(e)

When a single vowel is followed by a single consonant and the word or syllable ends in a final e, usually the final e is _____ and the single vowel _____.

Give three example words which follow this pattern.

_____   _____   _____

3. CVVC

When two vowels are together in a word or syllable, frequently one vowel is _____ and the other is _____.

Give three example words which follow this pattern.

_____   _____   _____

Unit Four

4. CV & V Alone

When a word or syllable has only one vowel and that vowel comes at the end, usually the vowel is _____. A vowel alone usually has its _____ sound.

Have your instructor check your work.

Patterns   Pronunciation   Exercise 59

The following words are "nonsense" words. Look at the consonant- vowel pattern. Mark the vowel sounds short, long, or silent. Pronounce the words to yourself. Turn off the tape while you read. Then turn on the tape, listen to the correct pronunciations, and circle your errors.

1. rin	2. bline	3. plean	4. mo	5. hab	6. cabe
7. scraim	8. si	9. fos	10. spose	11. groab	12. j i
13. lel	14. grele	15. zay	16. re	17. ux	18. mune
19. fleer	20. pu				

Patterns   Pronunciation   Exercise 60

Names of people frequently do not conform to the C-V patterns. Assume the ones below do. The names are divided into syllables for you. Look at the pattern in each syllable. Mark the vowels long (−), short (⌣), or silent (/). Then pronounce the name. After you have practiced, check your pronunciations with your tutor or instructor.

Example: Miss Ve̅e¢k
Mr. Kĕt
Mrs. Du̅l¢
Mr. Sisgivink   Sĭs gĭv ĭnk

1. Mrs. Fum
2. Mr. Bap
3. Mr. Mo
4. Miss Pame
5. Ms. Taze
6. Mr. Krendo   Kren do
7. Mr. Smeeknon   Smeek non
8. Miss Hinlok   Hin lok
9. Mrs. Pijmin   Pij min
10. Mr. Bupsule   Bup sule

Unit Four

11. Mr. Wone
12. Mr. Rinhipe   Rin hipe

Listen as the directions are read for the following application exercises. Then have your work checked before continuing the unit.

APPLICATION 1: UNIT FOUR   CONSONANT-VOWEL PATTERNS

From your reading find five words you cannot pronounce. Write them on the numbered blanks below. On the blank lines below each word, write the sentence in which you found the word. Then follow the directions below.

1. _____

   _____
   _____

2. _____

   _____
   _____

3. _____

   _____
   _____

4. _____

   _____
   _____

5. _____

   _____
   _____

Unit Four

Use C-V pattern to identify each word. Do it this way:

1. Underline each vowel you see in the word.

    Examples: banjo   polecat

2. Circle the C-V pattern you see around each vowel.

    Examples: (ban)(jo)   (pole)(cat)

3. Give the vowels the sound you would expect to hear in the pattern you see. Mark each vowel long (−), short (⌣), or silent (/).

    Example: (băn)(jō)   (pōlé)(căt)

4. Put consonant and vowel sounds together. Try to pronounce each syllable, and then the whole word.

    Example: bănjō   Is this a familar word?
                              Or, is it close to a word you know?

    Try pōlécăt   Say it quickly several times.
                              Does it sound like a word you know?

    If not, try a schwa sound in a sylllable.

5. Reread the sentence in which you found the word. Pronounce the word to yourself as you read. Think about the idea in the sentence. Does the word make sense in the sentence?

Do the best you can. Some words will be difficult for you. Do not worry if you cannot pronounce each one. Go over your work with your instructor.

UNITS OF SOUND

Skill Lesson an en un ilt op ut Exercise 61

Some C-V patterns occur frequently in words. Watch for them as units, or chunks, of sound.

Example: g<u>un</u> Recognizing the "un sound helps you quickly pronounce other -un words:

bun   stunt   punter   funny

In the word at the top of each column below, look at the underlined chunk of sound. As each word in the column is pronounced, listen to the sound and underline the letters representing that sound:

f<u>an</u>	t<u>en</u>	w<u>ilt</u>	h<u>op</u>	b<u>ut</u>
chance	pen	stilt	shop	nut
mansion	suspend	built	flop	shut
caravan	sensible	kilt	stoppage	buttress

Check your answers with the Key.

an en un ilt op ut Exercise 62

As each word below is pronounced on the tape, listen for the sound units within the word. In the blank, write the unit you hear:

an, en, un, ilt, op, ut

Example: b _ut_ ler ch _op_ per t _en_ t

1. f____er   2. m____tion   3. st____dard   4. p____over   5. sc____tleb____t

6. st____ned   7. b____ner   8. sh____t   9. k____er   10. cont____tm____t

11. bl____t   12. ____tional   13. S____skrit   14. ch____per

15. g____r____ner   16. ____b____ton   17. f____ration   18. n____nery

Check your answers with the Key.

Unit Four

at   Exercise 63

In the first line of the columns below, look at the word bat then look across and read cat, chat, and mat. The at occurs in each word. The sound "at" remains the same. By substituting, or putting, c, ch, or m in place of b in bat, a new word is formed. The words in each column have the "at" sound. As each word is pronounced, listen to the "at" sound in the word. Underline at:

bat	cat	chat	mat
battery	catalog	chatter	matter
batting	caterpillar	Chattanooga	matinee
battle	cattle	Chatham	matrimony

Check your answers with the Key.

ad   Exercise 64

Sustitute consonants with another unit of sound: ad

Write the word mad   *mad*
Cross out the m   *m̸ad*
Drop the m and write s in its place   *sad*
Pronounce the new word: sad.

In the spaces below, substitute consonants, digraphs, or consonant blends for the m in mad. Use consonants that make real words that are familiar to you.

Examples: glad   fad.

1._____   2._____   3._____   4._____   5._____

6._____   7._____   8._____   9._____   10._____

Check your answers with possible answers in the Key.

Some of your answers may not be in the Key; have your instructor check these.

Unit Four

atch Exercise 65

Notice longer units of sound which frequently occur in other words. For example: c<u>atch</u>. The "atch" sound is found in many words, such as l<u>atch</u> and m<u>atch</u>ing.

Listen carefully as the words below are pronounced. Repeat the word to yourself and underline the letters having the "atch" sound:

1. batch   2. hatchet   3. ratchet   4. catcher   5. scratch

In the blanks below write <u>atch</u> in the words having the "atch" sound. Some words have a different sound; put an <u>X</u> in those blanks.

    Example: h _atch_   wr _X_ ed

6. s____el   7. f____   8. p____y   9. m____

10. th____   11. p____work   12. cr____   13. m____maker

14. th____ing   15. th____ing

    Check your answers with the Key.

Remember: Units of sound that you see and hear often in words are

   an en un ilt op ut at ad atch

Each unit is the VC pattern and each has the short vowel sound you expect in that pattern. Watch for them.

However, sometimes you will see the CVC pattern, but the vowel will have its long, not short, sound. In the following exercises you will work with two of these units of sounds. Watch for these.

ight Exercise 66

The letters <u>ight</u> written together often do **not** conform to the consonant-vowel pattern sounds.
  Example: sl<u>ight</u> The letters i-g-h-t in a word are pronounced
      "ight." The <u>i</u> has its long, not short, sound.
As the following words are pronounced, repeat each to yourself and underline the <u>ight</u>:

1. night   2. brighten   3. daylight   4. delight   5. frightful

Unit Four

As the words below are pronounced, repeat each to yourself. Write <u>ight</u> in the blank of each word in which you hear "ight" as in <u>sight</u>. Put an <u>X</u> in the blank of each word in which you hear a different sound:

Example: s<u>*ight*</u> less   z <u>X</u> er

6. l_____ning   7. tw_____ter   8. t_____er   9. ins_____   10. fl_____

11. br_____er   12. br_____tle   13. m_____y   14. m_____le   15. r_____eous

Check your answers with the Key.

<u>old</u> Exercise 67

Another unit of sound which frequently does not conform to the vowel-consonant pattern is "old" as in <u>sold</u>.

As the following words are pronounced, repeat each to yourself, and underline the <u>old</u>:

1. gold   2. behold   3. told   4. soldier   5. boldness

As the words below are pronounced, repeat each to yourself. Write <u>old</u> in the blank of each word in which you hear "old" as in <u>sold</u>. Put an <u>X</u> in the blank of each word in which you hear a different sound.

Example: f <u>X</u> d   b <u>*old*</u> er

6. billf_____   7. up_____   8. sc_____   9. sc_____   10. b_____est

11. b_____   12. c_____   13. c_____   14. m_____y   15. s_____

Check your answers with the Key.

Review: To pronounce a word it is not always necessary to sound each letter.
1. Look for familiar units, or chunks, of sound that have the CV pattern. Most will have a short vowel sound.

Some are: <u>an</u>   <u>en</u>   <u>un</u>   <u>ilt</u>   <u>op</u>   <u>up</u>   <u>at</u>   <u>atch</u>

Write a word in which you see following patterns and hear the short vowel sound:

<u>an</u> _____   <u>en</u> _____   <u>un</u> _____

<u>ilt</u> _____   <u>op</u> _____   <u>ut</u> _____

<u>at</u> _____   <u>atch</u> _____

2. Watch for units of sound that have the VC pattern, but do **not** have the short vowel sound: <u>ight</u> and <u>old</u>.

   Write one example word for each: _____ _____.
   Have your instructor check your Review.

Using sound patterns is one of several ways to pronounce words. They do not always work. You must think about what words tell you. Pronouncing words is not reading; understanding ideas is reading.

APPLICATION 2: UNIT FOUR   UNITS OF SOUND

From other reading assignments, books, or magazines do the following exercises.

Find and write below ten words in which you see <u>an</u>. Circle each word having the short <u>a</u> sound:

1. _____   2. _____   3. _____   4. _____   5. _____

5. _____   6. _____   7. _____   8. _____   10. _____

Find and write below ten words in which you see <u>en</u>. Circle each word having the short <u>e</u> sound:
1. _____   2. _____   3. _____   4. _____   5. _____

5. _____   6. _____   7. _____   8. _____   10. _____

Find and write below ten words in which you see <u>un</u>. Circle each word having the short <u>u</u> sound:
1. _____   2. _____   3. _____   4. _____   5. _____

5. _____   6. _____   7. _____   8. _____   10. _____

Summary:
You know the the short, long, and schwa vowel sounds.

You recognize C-V patterns where you usually hear the short and long vowel sounds. You understand that in words with more than one syllable, you may hear a schwa vowel sound on an unaccented syllable.

There are additional ways vowel sounds change. You will work with these sounds in the following exercises. Before continuing, discuss your work and your questions with your instructor.

ADDITIONAL VOWEL SOUNDS

Skill Lesson   R-Affected Vowels   Exercise 68

If a vowel is followed by r, the sound of the vowel is almost always changed. As each pair of words is pronounced, repeat both words to yourself and listen to the vowel sounds:

    am   arm   The a in am has the short sound.
                            The a in arm is not the short, long, nor schwa sound.

    skit   skirt   not   North   hem   her

    hen   here   bun   burn   flit   flirt

However, you cannot count on r-affected vowels always having the same sound. Listen to the different sounds of the e in these words:

                    here   where   were

Many of the r-affected vowel words you already recognize; others will become familiar to you.

When you pronounce new words:

    1. Notice ar, er, ir, or, ur combinations

    2. Remember, the vowel followed by an r will not have a short or long sound.

Listen as the following words are pronounced. Repeat each to yourself. Mark each vowel either long (−), short (⌣), r-affected (R), or silent (/).

            Example: click   clerk   remark

1. pat   2. part 3. phone 4. form 5. cut 6. cure 7. jar   8. jam

9. very 10. rare 11. pen   12. per 13. car 14. can 15. nun 16. nurse

17. grow 18. got 19. curve 20. hurry
              Check your answers with the Key.

Note: If the r comes after the vowel, it changes the vowel sound; however, if the r comes before a vowel, it does not change the vowel sound. Examples:

no r	r before the vowel	r after the vowel
pays	praise	pairs
Fay	fray	far
tap	trap	tarp
bid	bridge	bird

QUIZ   R-Affected Vowels   Exercise 69

Mark each vowel either long (−), short (∪), r-affected (R), or silent (/):

Example: grāvé cărp hăppȳ

1. fun   2. fur   3. ladder   4. grand   5. sharp   6. lad   7. large

8. fern   9. fee   10. lard   11. bird   12. bid   13. ban   14. barn

15. fame   16. fare   17. grubby   18. curb   19. here   20. fort

Have your instructor check your quiz at the end of this unit.

In Unit Two you learned that alphabet letters represent speech sounds, and that in our English speech there are more sounds than the twenty-six letters in our alphabet. When we write words, these other sounds are shown by combinations of letters. You worked with digraphs, a combination of consonant letters, that stand for new consonant sounds.

You will now work with combinations of vowel letters which represent vowel sounds that flow into one another. These vowel sounds are called diphthongs. The most common diphthongs are:

oi	and	oy	as in	oil and boy
ou	and	ow	as in	found and cow
au	and	aw	as in	auto and lawn
oo			as in	bloom

Unit Four

Skill Lesson   Diphthongs oi-oy   Exercise 70

Usually oi and oy written together are pronounced as in the words oil and boy.
        Examples: joint   foil   joy   convoy

Listen as the following oi and oy words are pronounced. Underline the words that have the same sound as in oil and boy.
        Example: boil   joy

1. broiler   2. decoy   3. poison   4. coin   5. avoid   6. join   7. uncoil   8. loyal

9. moisture   10. soy   11. oyster   12. typhoid   13. Roy   14. boyish   15. soil
        Check your answers with the Key.

Note: Some rare oi words are not pronounced with the "oi" sound:
        coincide is pronounced   co-in-cide
        coinsure is pronounced   co-in-sure
        coiffure is pronounced   kwo-fyu(ə)r

    These are **not** diphthongs.

Skill Lesson   Diphthongs ou-ow   Exercise 71

Frequently, ou and ow combinations are pronounced as in found and cow.

        Examples: around   flour   Howard   powder

However, sometimes the ou and ow combinations have different sounds. These are **not** diphthongs.
        Examples: snow   shoulder   precious

Listen as the following ou and ow words are pronounced. Circle the words that have the same sound as in found and cow. Not all words will be circled.

        Example: (how)   show   gracious   (flour)

1. powwow   2. blown   3. bounce   4. shout   5. could   6. shower   7. cough   8. sprout

9. grouchy   10. your   11. lawnmower   12. blouse   13. spacious   14. couch   15. gown
        Check your answers with the Key.

Note: w is a vowel in a diphthong. It is part of a vowel sound.

QUIZ oi-oy and ou-ow Exercise 72

Listen carefully as the words below are pronounced. Underline the oi-oy words having the same sound as in oil and boy. Circle the ou-ow words having the same sound as in found and cow. Not all words will be marked. Follow the directions carefully.

Example: (scow) pointed   double   joyless

1. growl   2. cousin   3. pound   4. join   5. throw   6. coinsure   7. hoist

8. coyly   9. noise   10. mountain   11. county   12. country   13. pronounce

14. glowing   15. destroy

Have your quiz checked at the end of this unit.

Skill Lesson ô Diphthong Exercise 73

The symbol ô is used in the dictionary to represent the vowel sound you hear in saw and taught. Listen to the ô sound in the following words:

draw   cost   Paul   talk

Notice the letter combinations that have the ô sound:

auto   lawn   tall   lost

Sometimes these same letter combinations do **not** have the ô sound; they are not diphthongs.

laugh   away   pal   lot

As the following words are pronounced, repeat each word to yourself. Underline the words in which you hear the ô sound. Listen carefully for the sound you hear.

Example: bald   alert   caught   calcium

1. audience   2. fraud   3. chalk   4. ballet   5. auto   6. cough

7. rough   8. waltz   9. auction   10. calf   11. lawn   12. auger

13. boss   14. awake   15. sauce   16. half   17. nautical   18. palace

19. alcohol   20. though

Check your answers with the Key.

Unit Four

QUIZ ô Diphthong   Exercise 74

Underline the words in which you hear the ô sound.

Example: alas   walk   awning

1. brawl 2. wallet 3. August 4. Pawnee 5. moss 6. malted
7. away 8. vault 9. dawn 10. gauze 11. Australia 12. gauge
13. chalk 14. mallet 15. calendar

Have your quiz checked when you complete this unit.

Skill Lesson oo Diphthong   Exercise 75

The oo letter combination can have four different sounds:
- oo as in bloom
- oo as in book
- oo as in door
- oo as in blood

This appears confusing at first. However, it is less puzzling when you understand that the first sound is the most common:

oo as in bloom. You hear it in smooth, goofy, racoon

The second sound is less common, but is often found in the ook words:
oo as in book. You hear it in took, shook, look, and in wood, foot, good.

The last two oo sounds occur infrequently. You can think of these as exceptions:
oo as in door occurs in floor, doorway
oo as in blood occurs in flood.

These exceptions are common words you may already know how to pronounce. If not, as your reading progresses you will soon recognize and pronounce them on sight. Or, you may quickly figure out the word from the meaning of the sentence. When you need sound clues to help you pronounce oo words, remember:
First, try the bloom sound.
Then, try the book sound.
Next, try the door sound.
Then, try the blood sound.

Again, a memory aid is helpful. Visualize this picture; it helps you remember the clue words for the oo sounds:

Listen as the words below are pronounced. Underline the words that have the same sound you hear in bloom.

                    Example: look   room   doorstep

1. boot   2. zoo   3. foot   4. brushwood   5. brooch

6. bridegroom   7. lookout   8. bloodshed   9. pool   10. noose

11. bamboo   12. redwood   13. cocoon   14. noonday   15. igloo

                Check your answers with the Key.

QUIZ oo Sounds   Exercise 76

Listen as the words below are pronounced. Underline the words that have the same sound you hear in bloom.

                   Example: foot   groove   blood

1. gloomy   2. girlhood   3. stool   4. floodlight   5. took

6. bootleg   7. snoopy   8. bassoon   9. look   10. rooster

               Have your instructor check all your quizzes.

Unit Four

Note: The oo sound is often made with ew or ue:

    new   drew   slew   blue   clue   true

REVIEW: UNIT FOUR   ADDITIONAL VOWEL SOUNDS

You may refer to the previous exercises if you need help answering the review questions.

The most common vowel sounds are short, long, and schwa. However, vowel sounds are changeable. When you pronounce new words, watch for pairs of vowel letters that represent other vowel sounds.

1. **A vowel followed by an r may sound as in tar, her, mirror, or curve.**
   Write five words that have r-affected vowels:

   ar_____   er_____   ir_____

   or_____   ur_____

   Remember, they may not always sound the same: her, where, and here.

2. **An a followed by u, w, or l may sound as in caught, caw, or call.**
   Write three other example words:

   au_____   aw_____   al_____

3. **Some pairs of vowels often have a sound that is different than when each vowel is pronounced separately:**

   oi may sound as in oil; oy may sound as in boy.

       Write an example word for each: _____, _____.

   ou may sound as in found; ow may sound as in cow.

       Write an example word for each: _____, _____.

   oo may sound as in bloom, book, door, or blood.

       Write an oo word that sounds like bloom: _____.
           Have your instructor check your work.

APPLICATION 3: UNIT FOUR   ADDITIONAL VOWEL SOUNDS

From your other reading assignments find and underline words that have these letter combinations:

<u>oi</u> <u>oy</u> <u>ou</u> <u>ow</u> <u>au</u> <u>aw</u> <u>al</u> <u>oo</u>

After you complete your assignment write four words in each section below. After each word write the page number on which you found the word. Example: loudly (91). Then follow the directions given.

A.   Write four <u>ou</u> or <u>ow</u> words.

   1. _____   2. _____   3. _____   4. _____

   Circle the words that sound like <u>found</u> and <u>cow</u>.
   If you are not sure how to pronounce a word, try the "ow" sound, then reread the sentence.
   Does the word make sense?
      If it does, circle it;
      If it does not, continue your work.

B.   Write four <u>oi</u> or <u>oy</u> words:

   1. _____   2. _____   3. _____   4. _____

   Circle the words that have the same sound as in <u>oil</u> and <u>boy</u>.
   If you cannot pronounce a word, try the "oi" sound.
   Reread the sentence. Does the word make sense?
      If it does, circle it;
      If it does not, continue your work.

C.   Write four <u>au</u> <u>aw</u> <u>al</u> words:

   1. _____   2. _____   3. _____   4. _____

   Circle the words having the same sound as <u>saw</u>.
   If you cannot pronounce a word, try the "aw" sound and reread the sentence.
   Does the word make sense?
      If it does, circle it;
      If it does not, continue your work.

Unit Four

D.   Write four oo words:

1. _____ 2. _____ 3. _____ 4. _____

Circle the words having the same sound as in bloom.
If you cannot pronounce a word, try the "oo" sound and reread the sentence.
Does the word make sense?
    If it does, circle it;
    If it does not, continue.
        Have your instructor check your work.

SYLLABICATION

Skill Lesson Body of the Word Exercise 77

A student who had gone through survival school told his class how to cook grasshoppers: You remove the head, remove the legs, remove the wings. What you have left you can roast and eat. That's about the way you can break words into syllables:

>Remove the prefix
>Remove the suffix

What you have left you can eat. Well, at least you can break it down and pronounce it.

In the previous exercises, words of more than one syllable were divided for you. Now, how can you break down the body of the word into syllables?

1. Examine the body of the word. Ignore all the consonants, including the consonant blends and consonant digraphs, until you get to the first vowel:

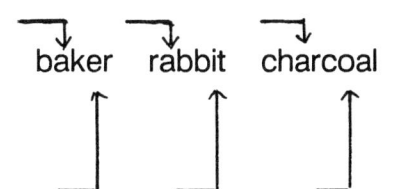

>baker rabbit charcoal

2. Look for the next vowel.

3. Then follow two basic rules:

   A. When you see <u>one consonant between vowels,</u> divide <u>before</u> the consonant: (V/CV)

   >baker baker ba-ker

   B. When you see <u>two consonants between vowels,</u> divide <u>between</u> the consonants: (VC/CV)

   >rabbit rabbit rab-bit

   >charcoal charcoal char-coal

   Other Examples.

V/CV:	pi-lot	clo-ver	di-ver	gla-zier	ty-pist
VC/CV:	pot-ter	ser-vant	frog-man	run-ner	ac-tor

Unit Four

Break the following words into two syllables using the V/CV rule. Pronounce each word. Turn off the tape while you work.

Example: ba|con   ba-con

1. cozy _____ 2. femur _____ 3. lotus _____

4. native _____ 5. provoke _____

The first syllable ends with a vowel. Did you give that vowel its long sound? Listen and check your pronunciation.

Break the following words into two syllables using the VC/CV rule. Pronounce each word. Turn off the tape while you work.

Example: gar|den   gar-den

6. Angels _____ 7. Yankees _____ 8. Broncos _____

9. Phillies _____ 10. Bengals _____

The vowel in the first syllable is between consonants. Did you give that vowel its short sound? Listen and check.

Break the following words into two syllables using either the V/CV or VC/CV rule. Divide each word; then pronounce it. Turn off the tape while you work.

11. Tigers _____ 12. parrot _____ 13. dopa _____

14. Padres _____ 15. ember _____ 16. emir _____

17. dormer _____ 18. emcee _____ 19. homburg _____

20. murder _____

Say the words again as you listen to the pronunciations.

Note: These two rules are good, but they do not work all the time:
   river is not pronounced ri-ver
   lemon is not pronounced le-mon
When a word sounds strange, divide <u>after</u> the consonant:
   riv-er   lem-on

No rule in English works all the time. When you have to pronounce a strange word, first try to break it into syllables; then use your phonic skills to pronounce each syllable.

Unit Four

Syllabication   Removing the Prefix   Exercise 78

A **prefix** is a word part attached to the beginning of a real word to change its meaning:

Unhappy is not the same as happy
Rewrite is not the same as write.
Disconnect is not the same as connect.
Prewar is not the same as war.
Misread is not the same as read.

Un, re, dis, pre, and mis are all prefixes. There are many more. You will learn to recognize them as you read. Good readers are very aware of prefixes. Start noticing them.

Remove the prefixes from the following words. Then examine the base word to see if it can be broken into two syllables. If it can, then divide it using the V/CV or VC/CV rule. The first two are done for you.

1. replace   re-place
2. resurface   re-sur-face
3. uneven

4. unhappy
5. disfavor
6. unending

7. disinfect
8. misfortune
9. discolor

10. mislead
11. prearrange
12. misdirect

13. precancerous
14. reinforce
15. preconceive

Check your answers with the Key.

Unit Four

Syllabication Removing the Suffix Exercise 79

Suffixes are found at the ends of words. They are used a lot, but they do not do much. They usually change a word to a different part of speech; that is, they make the word do a different job in a sentence:

Press your pants.
Check the pressure in the right front tire.
   -ure changed press from an action word to a naming word.

The magnet picked up all the nails.
The magnetic compass was faulty.
   -ic changed magnet from a naming word to a describing word.

Part of the stadium is filled
The stadium is partly full.
   -ly changed part from a naming word to a describing word.

Cotton shirts absorb perspiration better than nylon shirts.
Absorbent shirts are comfortable.
   -ent changes absorb from an action word to a describing word.

The suffixes ure, ic, ly and ent changed the words to different parts of speech in their sentences.

Underline the suffixes you see in the words below.

Naming word suffixes: ance or ist ment ness

   1. agreement   2. actor   3. stubborness   4. importance   5. artist

Action word suffixes: ate en ify ize

   6. broaden   7. energize   8. activate   9. glorify

Describing word suffixes: ant ful ish ous y

   10. careful   11. moldy   12. ignorant   13. delicious   14. childish
         Check your answers with the Key.

QUIZ   Syllabication   Exercise 80

Twelve words are given below. Some have one syllable, some have two, some have three.
First, turn off the tape; divide each word into syllables, and write them on the lines below. Then turn on the tape again.

Irish   melon   Norton   motor   college   fippenny

Muskegon   gland   twelve   gizmo   temper   murmur

Write the one-syllable words:

_____   _____

Write the two-syllable words:

_____   _____

_____   _____

_____   _____

_____   _____

Write the three-syllable words:

_____   _____

Now, listen as all the questions in this quiz are read. Then, come back to Question 1 and answer each question. Turn off the tape while you work.

1. Which two words follow the V/CV rule? _____ _____

2. Which word breaks the V/CV rule? _____

3. Which five two-syllable words follow the VC/CV rule?

   _____ _____ _____ _____ _____

4. Which three-syllable word follows this rule: VC/CV/C? _____

5. Which three-syllable word follows this rule: VC/CVC/CV? _____

       Have your instructor check your quiz.

Unit Four   85

Remember: If you do not know a word try to identify it as quickly as you can.

1. Think about what word makes sense in the sentence.

2. Look for familiar units of sound.

3. Try the consonant sounds in the word.

4. Look for the consonant-vowel patterns.

5. Try the vowel sounds.

    -Watch for r-affected vowels.

    -Watch for vowel combinations.

    -Watch for prefixes and suffixes.

Use whatever clues work for you.

Push ahead; hold onto the ideas you read.

Evaluate your Unit Four work with your instructor. In Unit Five you will combine meaning and sounds.

APPLICATION 4: UNIT FOUR   SYLLABICATION

Words You Can Pronounce

From your reading assignment find six words of more than one syllable that you **can** pronounce. Underline each.

After you complete your assignment, write the words on the numbered lines below (Whole word: _____).
Divide each word this way:
  1. Remove the prefix.
  2. Remove the suffix.
  3. Divide the body into syllables.

If cannot identify the prefix or suffix, look through the whole word, and apply the V/CV and VC/CV rules.

Examples: pas/sen/ger   un/der/line   re/peat

After dividing the word, pronounce it according to the rules. Then pronounce it as you say it in speech and compare the sounds.

1. Whole word: _____
   Prefix _____
   Suffix _____
   Word in syllables _____

2. Whole word: _____
   Prefix _____
   Suffix _____
   Word in syllables _____

3. Whole word: _____
   Prefix _____
   Suffix _____
   Word in syllables _____

4. Whole word: _____
   Prefix _____
   Suffix _____
   Word in syllables _____

5. Whole word: _____
   Prefix _____
   Suffix _____
   Word in syllables _____

6. Whole word: _____
   Prefix _____
   Suffix _____
   Word in syllables _____

Have your instructor check your work.

APPLICATION 5: UNIT FOUR   SYLLABICATION

Words You Cannot Pronounce

From your reading assignment find six words of more than one syllable that you **cannot** pronounce. Underline each.

After you complete your reading, write them below on the numbered lines below. (Whole word: _____).

Divide each word this way:
1. Remove the prefix.
2. Remove the suffix.
3. Divide the body into syllables.

If you are unable to identify a prefix or suffix, try dividing the whole word by looking through the whole word and applying the V/CV and VC/CV rules.

Examples: pas/sen/ger   un/der/line   re/peat

After dividing the word, pronounce it according to the rules. Then pronounce it as you say it in speech and compare the sounds.

1. Whole word: _____
   Prefix _____
   Suffix _____
   Word in syllables _____

2. Whole word: _____
   Prefix _____
   Suffix _____
   Word in syllables _____

3. Whole word: _____
   Prefix _____
   Suffix _____
   Word in syllables _____

4. Whole word: _____
   Prefix _____
   Suffix _____
   Word in syllables _____

5. Whole word: _____
   Prefix _____
   Suffix _____
   Word in syllables _____

6. Whole word: _____
   Prefix _____
   Suffix _____
   Word in syllables _____

Have your instructor check your work.

UNIT FIVE

COMBINING PHONICS AND CONTEXT CLUES

STUDENT NOTES

UNIT FIVE: COMBINING PHONICS AND CONTEXT CLUES

Skill Lesson   Background Knowledge Clues   Exercise 81

In the first four units of Basic Phonics for Adults you used phonic analysis to figure out words you did not know. Because phonics alone does not always work, you were reminded to pay attention to the meanings and ideas you read. Ideas give valuable clues for identifying words. These are called context clues. "Context" refers to the surrounding words, pictures, and ideas from which you get the clues. To use context clues you must understand what the selection tells you, think about it in your own words, then connect it to what you already know.

The first exercises using context clues will offer no phonics clues at all. For some exercises in this unit there can be more than one correct answer for a question, so there are no Key answers for you to check. Think about what makes sense and what is familiar to you. Use your imagination; guess. Your instructor will go over your work with you when you have completed the unit. If you have questions as you work, ask your instructor or tutor for help.

This unit teaches three kinds of context clues:
1. Background knowledge clues
2. Sentence structure clues
3. Paragraph idea clues.

Background knowledge clues come from the experiences in your life. School, friends, television, radio, newspapers, and magazines have given you many kinds of information and ideas; you have a wealth of background knowledge. While you read, think about the ideas in the selection. When you come to a word you do not know ask yourself, "From what I already know, what might this word be?"

> Example: Tom told the joke about the yellow alligator; Kate _____ till tears came to her eyes.
> From experience you know that good jokes are humorous and cause laughter, so you might guess that the missing word is "laughed". What other words would make sense? _____, _____

In each sentence below one word is missing. Read the whole sentence; skip over the blank. Think about the idea of the sentence. From your background knowledge, what word would make sense? Write it in the first blank. Think of two other words which also fit. Write them in the remaining blanks.

Example: Carol was _angry/upset/worried_ ; her date was two hours late.

1. While soaking in her bubble bath, Marsha heard the telephone ringing, but she

    could not _____ it.
    _____

2. Harper _____ one into left field but it curved foul.

3. Clark did not want to go to the party when he heard that his _____ would be there.

4. The police officer spotted the _____ window and knew something was wrong.

5. It worried my neighbor to leave his _____ at home alone.

Skill Lesson   Sentence Structure Clues: Naming Words
Exercise 82

Context clues can be found in **sentence structure**, that is, from the way words are arranged in a sentence. When you come to a word you do not recognize, think about what kind of word would make sense in that particular place in the sentence. Read the whole sentence up to the period (.), question mark (?), or exclamation mark (!) which marks the end of it.

Each word in a sentence has a specific purpose or job. Some words **name** a person, place, thing, or idea.

Example: Eric's grandparents, the first to arrive for dinner, parked their _____ in the driveway. The missing word names something the grandparents are driving or riding. It could be car, van, Oldsmobile, or buggy. Add two more words which make sense: _____, _____.

92

Unit Five

In each sentence below a **naming** word is missing. Listen as each sentence is read. Write in the blank a word which makes sense.
   Example: From the dessert _cart_ Arthur selected peach pie.

1. In the history section of the library, Henry found three books about the _____ of the Civil War.

2. _____ from the Goaded Goat Band rocked the recreation room.

3. Ginger saved her money for three years in order to buy a new _____ and then piled it up on the freeway driving it home.

4. Tillie forgot to put the _____ in the refrigerator before she went on vacation, but she smelled her mistake when she stepped in the house.

5. Ten-Gallon Tyler ordered another cold _____ to go with the red hot _____.

Skill Lesson   Sentence Structure Clues: Action Words
Exercise 83

Some words in the sentence tell what is taking place, or what **action** is occurring.

   Example: After baking her brains in the sun for three hours watching the Tigers drop another double-header, Laurie _____ two bottles of Coke and a Mexican beer.
   The missing word in this sentence must be an action word telling what Laurie did with the Coke and the beer. She may have "gulped" or "ordered" them. What other word makes sense? _____

In each sentence below an action word is missing. Listen as each sentence is read. Write in the blank a word which makes sense.
   Example: The heavens rumbled, the rain _poured_, and the flood waters rose.

1. Before leaving for Alaska, JoAnn _____ the shelves of the motor home with baked beans and chicken-rice soup.

2. The prisoners _____ the escape for early morning.

3. All four women _____ about the problems of women in management.

Unit Five

4. "I'm sorry," cried Olga, "I could never marry a man who would _____ a dumb animal!"

5. Harvey _____ sports cars, speed boats, and girls in lavender running shoes.

Skill Lesson   Sentence Structure Clues: Describing Words
Exercise 84

Some words **describe** a person, place, thing, or an action.
   Example: Walter filled the sky with shot and brought home feathers; Walter was an _____ duck hunter.
   The missing word in this sentence will **describe** the kind of duck hunter Walter was. Since he filled the sky with shot and came home without a duck we may assume he was an _____ hunter. (unskilled, unhappy, untrained, unsuccessful, inexperienced, ignorant.)
   Note: Be sure your word starts with a, e, i, o, or u. If a noun starts with a vowel we say "an ____"; if it begins with a consonant we say "a ____". We say "an apple", but we say "a bannana."

In each sentence below the missing word is one which describes. Listen as each sentence is read. From the four words below the sentence, select the one which makes the most sensible sentence. Write that word in the blank. Only one answer is correct.
   Example: In the _stuffy_ classroom Mike could barely stay awake.
      sunny   cold   stuffy   noisy

1. During _____ vacation the Carters joined a caroling group and sang three nights a week in nursing homes.
      spring   Christmas   Easter   Labor Day

2. Because you write so _____ you had better type your papers.
      clearly   carelessly   carefully   expertly

3. The beige, _____ boots, carefully hand-tooled, were the most expensive.
      leather   vinyl   cloth   fuzzy

4. Herb shouted _____ at the boys pelting snowballs at his terrier.
      softly   happily   carefully   angrily

5. The _____ woman pointed her cane toward the bowl of milk and croaked, "Here Kitty".
      screaming   giggling   young   stooped
   Check your answers with the Key.

Unit Five

Sentence Structure Clues: Naming, Action, Describing Words
Exercise 85

Each sentence below has a missing word which **names**, **describes**, or tells **action**. In each blank write a word that makes sense. There may be many possible answers.

Example: Claybourne ate his *tossed* salad while he waited for his sizzler.

1. Al lassoed and threw the _____.

2. The listing boat _____ toward Muskegon, the nearest port.

3. I like a glass of cold milk with a _____ sandwich.

4. Seeing Blair's new haircut, Chuck was dissatisfied with his own _____ hair.

5. Rosie _____ in the doorway and looked back at the car parked at the curb.

Skill Lesson   Phonics and Context   Exercise 86

In the previous context clue exercises you found that more than one word often makes sense in a sentence. To more accurately identify a particular word, add your phonics skills to the context clues. For example, in the sentence "The robin flew into the _____", several words - tree, grass, woods - make sense. If you add sounds of letters to the idea of the sentence you can better identify the word.

　　　　Example: The robin flew into the w_____ow.
　　　　The robin flew into the y_____d.
　　　　The robin flew into the b_____sh.
　　　　The robin flew into the (<u>window, yard, bush</u>).

When a word puzzles you, hang onto the sentence meaning while you look through the word and sound the consonants. This alone may give you the word. If it does not, add sounds of vowels, vowel combinations, or familiar units of sound. Think about vowel-consonant patterns.

In the exercises below combine sense and sound to identify the word. Write the word in the blank at the end of the sentence. This exercise is not on tape. Use your own inner voice to help you read the sentences. Do not be concerned about reading aloud. Go ahead and read it out loud if it helps you, but do it softly. Turn off the tape while you work.

Unit Five

Example:
  The marathon route ran along the p__rk. *park*
  The marathon route ran along the b_ch. *beach*
  The marathon route ran along the r__er. *river*

1. Dark, cold weather often makes a person feel t_r_d. _____

2. Dark, cold weather often makes a person feel gl__my. _____

3. Dark, cold weather often makes a person feel d_pr_ssed. _____

4. Dark, cold weather often makes a person feel m__dy. _____

5. The sign at the driveway warned "Pr_v_t_." _____

6. The sign at the driveway warned "No tr_sp_ss_ng." _____

7. The sign at the driveway warned "Be_w_r_ of d_g." _____

8. The sign at the driveway warned "Dr___ Sl__ly." _____
  Check your answers with the Key.

Phonics and Context Exercise 87

In the following sentences one word is incomplete. Select from the given units of sound one which makes a sensible word in the sentence. Turn the player off while you work.
  -ilt -op -atch -ight -old
  Example: Louie s*old* his catch of trout to the local restaurant.

1. By Thanksgiving, sh_____ windows all over the city were decorated for Christmas.

2. A slang term once used to mean m_____es was "Lucifer," another name for the devil.

3. Loud claps of thunder fr_____ened the herd of half-wild Longhorns.

4. The thief b_____ly asked the guard for directions to the nearest exit.

5. I change my oil f_____er every time I change my oil: every three months.
  Check your answers with the Key.

Skill Lesson   Paragraph Idea Clues   Exercise 88

A last kind of context clue is the **paragraph idea** clue. A paragraph is a group of related sentences which deals with one particular point. You can recognize a paragraph because the first sentence is always indented, or set in, five spaces from the left margin of the page. (Look at the indentations at the beginning of the paragraphs in this unit.) Notice paragraphs while you read. A well-written paragraph is developed around one thought, idea, or topic. Winston Churchill began to write well only when he "began to see that writing...was not only an affair of sentences, but of paragraphs."

Churchill also noted that the paragraph, "just as the sentence, contains one idea in all its fullness." If you can locate that "one idea in all its fullness" you may be able to figure out words in that paragraph that you do not recognize. That "idea in all its fullness" may be either the topic or the main idea. The topic is usually one or two words; the main idea is usually a complete sentence. From the topic you can alert your mind to the type of words you might expect to read. This will, perhaps, help you figure out new words when you run into them.

There are two ways to locate the topic or the main idea:

(1) Look at the title of the paragraph IF IT HAS A TITLE.

(2) See where all the pronouns point.

Let's look at the first way, and assume a paragraph is titled: <u>A Summer Cookout</u>.

>   Example: If the paragraph topic is a summer cook-out you might expect words such as bonfire, charcoal, barbecue, weiners, shish kabobs, sirloin, mosquitoes, kosher dills, catsup, indigestion, poison ivy. Add three other words you might find in the paragraph about a summer cook-out.
>   _____, _____, _____

Think about each topic, then write four words you could expect in a paragraph written about that topic.

Example: national elections

vote   _conventions_   _delegates_   _candidates_

1. home computers

_____   _____   _____   _____

2. garden pests

_____   _____   _____   _____

Unit Five

3. a bank robbery

_____ _____ _____ _____ _____

4. Texas

_____ _____ _____ _____ _____

5. a tornado

_____ _____ _____ _____ _____

Skill Lesson   Paragraphs with Titles   Exercise 89

Before you read a paragraph, or selection, you can anticipate ideas from the title. Good readers do this:
1. Read the title
2. Think about the title
3. Guess what the selection is about

The following example leads you step-by-step through this process.

Step 1. **READ THE TITLE**.

Example: Read the title.

SELF-HYPNOSIS

Step 2. **THINK ABOUT THE TITLE**. What does it mean? Do you know about self-hypnosis? Write your thoughts and questions below.

_____

_____

_____

You may have written
-Is it was possible to hypnotize yourself?
-I have a friend who can hypnotize herself.
-How does one do this?
-Where does one learn self-hypnosis?
-How does one get back out of a self-hypnotic state?

Now, **read** the paragraph carefully. Try sense and sound to figure out the difficult or new words.

> The use of self-hypnosis is increasing. Doctors, dentists, and psychologists are teaching it to patients. It is helpful for overcoming fears and stress, insomnia, and pain. Some use it to control over-eating and to stop smoking. Illnesses, such as asthma and migraine are being effectively treated with self-hypnosis.

In the following paragraphs anticipate the topic. Read the title, think about the title, then guess what the paragraph is about. Write your guess in the line below the title.
Turn off the tape while you write.

INTERVIEW JITTERS

What do you think this paragraph will be about?

_____

Now read the paragraph and answer the questions.

> Mary was going to be interviewed for a new job. She was very nervous, but she wanted the computer sales job very badly. She tried to remember all she should do to make a favorable impression. Her resume was properly typed. She planned to dress conservatively in her navy blue suit. And she definitely intended to be on time. Now, if she could only control the nervous quiver in her voice.

Was the paragraph what you expected? _____

What was it about? _____

_____

_____

Do the same with the next paragraph.

DEAD MAN'S HAND

_____

> A pair of aces (or jacks) and a pair of eights in a poker hand is called a "dead man's hand." Wild Bill Hickock, a lawman, supposedly held these cards in a game when he was shot by Jack McCall in Deadwood, South Dakota in 1876. Poker players today consider it a lucky hand. In certain games it wins over even a royal flush.

Was the paragraph what you expected? _____

Unit Five

What was it about? _____

_____

Skill Lesson   Paragraphs without Titles   Exercise 90

REMEMBER: There are two ways to locate the topic of a paragraph.

1. **Look at the title if it has a title.**
2. **See where the pronouns point.**

We have dealt with paragraphs having titles. Most paragraphs, however, do not. What can you do then?

For one thing, as you read a paragraph, notice if a single name or word is repeated over and over. If it is, there is a good chance that the repeated word is part of the topic.

Also, look at the pronouns. Pronouns are such words as he, she, it, they, them, him, her. The pronouns often point to the topic.

Let's look at the first paragraph, the one about self-hypnosis. If it had no title we could read **watching to see where the pronouns point**.

> The use of self-hypnosis is increasing. Doctors, dentists, and psychologists are teaching **it** to patients. **It** is helpful for overcoming fears and stress, insomnia, and pain. Some use **it** to control over-eating and to stop smoking. Illnesses, such as asthma and migraine are being effectively treated with self-hypnosis.

Each **it** means "self-hypnosis."

Let's read another paragraph.

> The moccasin-toe is one of the most popular styles of men's shoes. **It** is soft, unlined, and usually found in loafer styles. **It** is actually an upside-down shoe. Most plain-toe, wing-tip, and dress slip-on shoes are made with the inside sole a separate piece of leather stitched to the sides of the shoe. The moccasin, however is just the reverse: **its** sole and sides are just one smooth piece of leather. An "apron" of leather is then hand-sewn to the sides to make the top piece of the shoe.

What is the topic? Look at all the **it** words: they all mean the moccasin-toe shoe. The topic is simply the moccasin-toe shoe.

Paragraphs without Titles   Exercise 91

Listen and follow as this paragraph is read:

Winding through sub-arctic wilderness, crawling over a mountain pass, crossing icy creeks and a vague national border, the Chilkoot Trail was a part of Alaskan history. Miners in 1898 followed it from the slap-dash seacoast village of Dyea into the Yukon. Each miner had to pack a thousand pounds of supplies on his back to get him through one year in the gold fields of the Klondike. They learned to hate all twenty-eight rugged miles of it. Most of the miners walked it thirty-nine times in order to pack in all their supplies. Jack London himself trod its stones and waded its streams. The Northwest Mounted Police tried to keep law and order on its Canadian section, but they were dealing with the innocent, the desperate, the greedy, and the murderous. And most of these people were armed. For almost a solid year it was the scene of a stormy free-for-all. But by 1900 it was deserted and grass grew over the bootprints. The gold rush was over; the buildings of Dyea were knocked down and hauled off to Skagway. The Chilkoot trail was abandoned by people, and only the bears left their tracks in its dust.

DIRECTIONS: RE-READ THE PARAGRAPH ABOVE AND CIRCLE THE WORD IT WHEREVER IT APPEARS. IN EVERY CASE IT REFERS TO THE TOPIC. TURN OFF THE PLAYER WHILE YOU READ.

WHAT IS THE TOPIC? _____

Check your answer with the Key.

Paragraphs without Titles   Exercise 92

Listen and follow as this paragraph is read.

The village of Talkeetna sits in the middle of Alaska. Perched on a railroad that runs between Fairbanks and Anchorage, nestled in between mountains and forest, and stuck at the end of a two-lane road, it seems to embody whatever Alaska stands for. Full of fiercely independent people who hold a moose-dropping festival every July, it contains one gas station, one road house, one leather works, one grocery store, one gold-and-antler trader, one dirt landing strip right smack in the middle of town, and one street. It does have two motels. But only one has numbers on the room. The other just has the doors painted in different colors. It has several bush pilots who make a living flying climbing parties up to Mt. McKinley and also buzzing tourists around snow-clad peaks scaring the daylights out of both the tourists and the mountain goats. It also has a few bars; it just wouldn't be Alaskan if there weren't a few bars.

DIRECTIONS: RE-READ THE PARAGRAPH ABOVE AND CIRCLE THE WORD IT WHEREVER IT APPEARS. THEY ALL REFER TO THE TOPIC OF THE PARAGRAPH. TURN OFF THE PLAYER WHILE YOU READ.

WHAT IS THE TOPIC? _____

Check your answer with the Key.

Combining Phonics and Context Clues   Exercise 93

Combining context clues and phonic clues is a challenging game. In spite of what some poor readers believe, good readers do not know all the words they run into; good readers do not automatically understand everything they read; good readers often have to guess about some things they read. What makes them good readers? They guess right. Learning how to use context clues and phonic clues may help you to learn to guess right also.

Now, how can you learn to guess correctly?

First, follow the clues you have already been given for examining the parts of a new word.

Second, if you can't figure out the new word yet, read beyond that word, well beyond it, in fact. Read the whole sentence; read the whole paragraph; read the whole page if you have to. And then come back to the mystery word and try a few pronunciations on it to see how they fit.

Third, be happy to almost know. You don't have to be absolutely sure of everything you read. "Almost knowing" is not a bad place to be.

To illustrate the Second Rule, consider this: If a sentence reads: "Early travelers wore g____s" we might not know whether they wore garters, gaiters, guns, or gloves. But if we read the rest of the phrase, "wore g____s or gauntlets on their hands," we would assume the mystery word to be "gloves."

If, in a discussion of material used to make tents seventy- five years ago, we read,

"Most of the tents were made of U.S. Army duck, flax, cotton, or waterproof b_ll__n silk", we might be confused. Could the missing word be "balloon"? The next sentence says,

"The term 'b_ll__n silk probably means the same material used in 'aerial balloons'...

So there it is, and it suddenly makes sense. Both of these examples appear in the next lessons.

Exercise 94

In the following exercises you will find "mystery words" which have missing letters. Read each sentence, trying to figure out the mystery word. When you have decided what word makes sense, fill in the missing letters. Some words may have more than one letter.

- If you know how to spell the word write in the correct letter, or letters.
- If you are not sure how to spell the word, write in the letter, or letters for the sound you hear.

Then re-read the entire sentence again just to make sure you are correct. Shut the player off until you have finished all four: <u>Henry Box Brown</u>, <u>Osa Johnson</u>, <u>Cloth for Clothes</u>, and <u>Tenting in 1910</u>.

HENRY BOX BROWN

In the 1850's a slave named Henry Brown was able to reach (1) fr__ _d_m in a most unusual manner: Mister Brown had (2) h_ms_lf boxed up in the slave city of Richmond, Virginia, and mailed to the free city of Philadelphia,(3) P__nnsylv__n__ __. He had friends to (4) h_lp him, of course. He (5)cl_mb_d into a tiny box only three feet by two feet, and only (6) thr__ __ feet long. Then his friends (7) n__ __l_d him inside and bound the box with hickory hoops.

Mr. Brown had with him a (8) c_nt__ __ner of water and a few biscuits. He was taken by dray to the (9)r__ __lr__ __d station and then loaded on board a (10) b_gg_g_ car. The baggage men could not read, (11)app__r__ntly, because, although the box was (12)l__b_l_d, "This Side Up", Mr. Brown (13)r_d_ on his head for part of the journey.

Unit Five

He arrived at (14) Ph__l__d__lph____ station two days after being loaded on the train, and was (15)t__k__n by wagon to the Anti-Slavery Office where a group of abolitionists anxiously awaited his (16)arr__v__l with a saw and hatchet. When the lid was pried loose, Mr. Brown rose from his box, (17)r__ __ch__d out his hand, and said, "How do you do?"

Samuel A. Smith, the white (18)fr__ __nd, who had (19)n__ __l__d him up and mailed him off, was (20)d__scov__r__d and sent to jail.

Check your answers with the Key.

Exercise 95

CLOTH FOR CLOTHES

We have many materials for (1)cl__th__ng today: (2)d__cr__n, polyester, vinyl, (3)n__l__n. But a glance at a 1910 Abercrombie and Fitch catalogue shows that many other (4)m__t__r__ __ls used to be made into (5)cl__th__ng. Back then there were Kersey trousers made of hard (6)w__ __l__n yarn spun over cotton thread, (7)c__rd__r__y trousers of English cloth, rubber (8)tr__ __s__rs for wearing in the wet, and oilskins for (9)h__ __vy rains. Some of the oilskins were made with (10)c__rd__r__y collars and genuine ivory (11)b__tt__ns. There were also shirts made of chamois (shammy) (12)l__ __th__r, the same material now used to make polishing cloths for washing cars, and there were even Swedish dogskin (13)j__ck__ts which were made, we may assume, out of genuine (14)Sw__d__sh dogs.

Check your answers with the Key.

Exercise 96

TENTING IN 1910

The 1910 A & F catalogue shows many (1)k__nds of tents for (2)c__mp__rs: waterproof (3)aut__m__b__le tents which were tied to the wooden spokes of a wheel; (4)r__fr__shm__nt tents (similar to modern "Beer Tents") made with bright awning stripes, some tents as small as 9 feet by 16, some as large as 25 feet by 50; garage tents to (5)pr__t__ct an open car; (6)c__mp__rtm__nt tents with four bedrooms; toilet tents which allowed "perfect privacy"; and a (7)ph__t__gr__ph__r's tent with a black-lined darkroom inside. A & F also sold many canoe tents which looked like (8)Ind__ __n teepees. Most of the tents were made of U.S.Army duck, flax, (9)c__tt__n, or waterproof (10)b__ll__ __n silk. The term "balloon silk" probably means the same (11)m__t__r__ __l used in "aerial balloons", the only way most people could travel through the air in 1910.

Check your answers with the Key.

Exercise 97

OSA JOHNSON

In the early (1)y__ __rs of the twentieth (2)c__nt__r__ there were adventurers and (3)expl__r__rs who made a living traveling to (4)str__ng__ and dangerous places and later giving talks and (5)p__ct__r__ shows (slides or (6)s__l__nt movies). One daring (7)adv__nt__r__r was a beautiful young lady (8)n__m__d Osa Johnson. Osa Leighty ran away from home and (9)m__rr__ __d the explorer, Martin Johnson when she was (10)s__xt__ __n years old. Osa and Martin sailed to the South (11)P__c__f__c, where they filmed cannibals and (12)h__ __dh__nt__rs at home before the natives were all disturbed and civilized by (13)J__p__n__s__ and (14)Am__r__c__n armed forces in World War Two. Martin (15)br__ __ght home several heads, (16)__ncl__d__ng, luckily, his own. The (17)J__hns__ns took dugout (18)c__n__ __s down snaky rivers in Borneo

Unit Five 105

and studied (19)or__ng__t__ns, gorillas, and (20)v__r__ __ __s other apes. They shot miles of film showing exotic animals and birds, as well as (21)n__t__v__ tribes who had never seen a white person before and kept trying to rub the (22)wh__t__ off their skins.

Osa built a home with Martin in (23)Afr__c__ where they made movies of (24)rh__n__c__r__s__s, elephants, lions, and all the varied (25)w__ldl__f__ in the (26)j__ngle and the grasslands. Martin (27)cr__nk__d the movie camera; Osa (28)gu__rd__d him with a .405 (29)W__nch__st__r, and sometimes she had to use it. Though hardly five feet (30)t__ll, Osa was a deadly shot with the (31)h__ __vy rifle and once dumped a (32)ch__rg__ng (33)rh__n__c__r__s at Martin's feet. However, it was a rare event when they shot an (34)att__ck__ng animal; usually they (35)cl__mb__d trees to (36)s__f__t__.

Although Osa would look a rampaging (37)__l__ph__nt in the eye, she was (38)t__rr__f__ __d of cobras, and she always wore high leather boots for (39)pr__t__ct__ __n against (40)sn__k__ bite. In her (41)f__ __r years in Africa she remained a lady of the 1920's: She took a (42)b__tht__b with her on all her (43)ov__rn__ght hikes, (44)c__v__r__d her face with cold (45)cr__ __m every night, and had her (46)h__ __r done once a day by a (47)s__rv__nt.

Her most (48)d__ng__r__ __s experience was coming down with (49)pn__ __m__n__ __ while (50)cl__mb__ng Mount Kenya. Martin's (51)cl__s__st call came when he blew himself up using ten-times too much old (52)f__sh__ __n__d flash powder for a (53)n__ght (54)ph__t__ of a whole (55)h__rd of (56)__l__ph__nts.

Osa recovered from the pneumonia, and Martin grew back his hair and skin. Their life together was filled with love and adventure until just before the war when Martin was killed in a plane crash.

Check your answers with the Key.

Note: After reading these selections you probably are still unsure of some words. Even expert readers cannot always pronounce every word nor understand precisely the meaning of each word. They frequently refer to a dictionary. The more you read the more you will find a dictionary useful to you.

QUIZ   Exercise 98

TRAVELING BY AUTO

Those who (1)tr_v_l_d by auto in 1910 needed special clothes and (2)eq___pm__nt. Both men and women wore long coats called "dusters" that (3)c_v_r_d them from neck to shoe-top. (4)D__st__rs were made of linen, "pongee" cloth, or mohair. (5)Tr__v__l__rs also wore (6)gl__v__s or gauntlets on their hands, leggins on their legs, and knee-high (7)b____ts on their feet. Caps and (8)h__ts kept the (9)h____r neat and the heads warm while heavy goggles (10)pr__t__ct__d the eyes. In winter travelers took (11)h____vy wool and silk (12)r__b__s for their laps, and often (13)incl__d__d footwarmers, which were flat stoves that (14)b__rn__d "coal bricks". For very cold (15)w____th__r they might wear a "visor hunting hood and muffler" (16)wh__ch we would call a ski (17)m__sk.

FOODS FOR CAMPING

Camping in 1910 meant (1)c__rry__ng interesting foods. There were cans of dehydrated (2)sp__n__ch, potatoes, (3)c__bb__g__, beans, and (4)b__rr____s. Campers might also purchase cans of pemmican (beef, dried fruit, and suet (5)p____nd__d into cakes), boxes of "hardtack" (6)br____d, and rolls of "pea-meal sausage." Campers (7)app__r__ntly liked tablets. There were tea tablets, soup tablets, bouillon tablets, and malted milk tablets.

Abercrombie and Fitch also sold (8)inst__nt coffee paste that came in (9)t__b__s like toothpaste. You just squeezed out a little (10)c__ff____ paste in your cup, added hot water, and you had (11)__nst__nt coffee.

Unit Five

Very bold campers tried meals in self-heating cans. These foods were in a can within a can. The (12)__ __t__r can was half-filled with quick-lime. (13)Add__ng water to the quick-lime created (14)a v__ __l__nt chemical reaction which raised the (15)t__mp__r__t__r__ of both cans very quickly. Too (16)q__ __ckly, sometimes, because the supper (17)occ__s__ __n__lly went off like a bomb and diners watched their New England boiled dinner, (18)Ir__sh stew, or Chicken Curry Indienne fly (19)thr__ __gh the pine trees to the astonishment of the squirrels.

Have your Quiz checked when you complete this unit.

CONGRATULATIONS

You have learned to use phonics and context clues to pronounce words. Practice your new skills on words you see on billboards, in television ads, on package labels, in newspapers and magazines, and in your assigned readings. With use, the new skills become automatic, and you become a comfortable reader.

You may want to review parts of this text. Research shows that reading something twice increases your comprehension. Reread the exercises for yourself, without the tapes. There are Additional Practices in the following section of the text. Your instructor can suggest other materials. Jot down your ideas and questions under Student Notes on page 111. Plan with your instructor what to study next.

Build onto these new skills. Recognizing more word parts - prefixes, roots, suffixes - will help you understand the meanings of words. At times, you will need to use the dictionary; using it efficiently makes reading easier for you. You probably want to read faster and concentrate better. In your notes add questions about these skills.

Remember, people read for new ideas and for fun.. . . . . what interests **you**? If you really want to read, go where books are kept. Go to your local public library.

Where is it?_____

What is the name of it?_____

Ask the librarian to tell you about the library:

    What do you have to do to get a library card?_____

_____

    How much does it cost?_____

    If you check out books on your card, how long can you keep them out?

_____

    What kinds of books <u>cannot</u> be checked out?_____

Why not go to the library every week?_____

    Which day?_____

Unit Five

STUDENT NOTES

Questions to ask the instructor:

What would I like to study next?

What would I like to read about?

Other thoughts and ideas:

Unit Five

ADDITIONAL EXERCISES
UNIT ONE

ALPHABET ORDER

A. Write each row of letters in alphabetical order.
            Example: w j z r f   *f j r w z*
1. s b q c m _____   2. g t v z a _____
3. r d n l e _____   4. j f o p h _____

B. Circle each of the following groups of letters that are in alphabetical order:
            Example: f h d s q   (d j n p r)
1. k r d p t   2. k m n p v   3. g u j l n   4. c o w v m
5. i c o j r   6. d m q s u   7. m g t v z   8. d e l n r
9. j h p o f   10. a f k s l w v

C. Write each row of words in alphabetical order:
    Example: pizza hamburgers eggs   *eggs hamburgers pizza*
1. minnow   rake   come: _____

2. fish   tank   lake: _____

3. leaves   jail   snow: _____

4. parent   very   got: _____

5. learn   write   memory: _____

D. Circle each group of words that is in alphabetical order:
            Example: let may can   (if so yet)
January December May   but do put   Mary Barb Laura

Saturday Tuesday Wednesday   Dan Kim Larry   tall short wide

CONSONANT-VOWEL RECOGNITION

A. Circle the vowels in the following row of letters: a t e s i h o p m r u

B. Underline each vowel letter you see in the groups of letters below. Circle the "sometimes vowels" y and w.
            Example: q <u>a</u> (y) b <u>e</u>
1. b e q r i   2. l o m a p y   3. z w i a u l r

4. a t i u r s e y z v i w   5. u e t a i y p t r a o

Additional Exercises

C. Write the vowel letters you see in each word below.

Example: dinner _i e_

1. splendid _____   2. animals _____   3. ghost _____

4. professor _____   5. disaster _____   6. wooden _____

D. Write the consonant letters you see in each word below.

Example: lunch _l nch_

1. forced _____ 2. classic _____ 3. giant _____ 4. hatrack _____

5. jungle _____ 6. evict _____ 7. excuse _____ 8. zipper _____

SUGGESTED PRACTICES
1. Select a sentence from a newspaper or magazine. Underline the vowel letters.
2. Begin with letter R (or K, etc.) and write the remainder of the alphabet in correct order.
3. In a newspaper or magazine article underline ten words. Write them in correct alphabetical order.
4. Write the names of five kinds of dogs; put them in alphabetical order.
5. Write the names of ten cities; put them in alphabetical order.

UNIT TWO

SOUNDS OF g
Below are pairs of g" words. In each pair, one word has a hard g sound; one word has a soft g sound. Circle the word that has the hard g sound.

Example: (gravy)   logical

generation gulf   urge   gallon   average Greek
change angle   knowledge program   segment German
grind gyrate   energy gain   grape gyp

SOUNDS OF c
Below are pairs of c words. In each pair, one word has a hard c sound; one word has a soft c sound. Circle the word that has the soft c sound.

Example: public   (police)

receive Coca Cola   education Greece   force electronic
acid metric   bacteria glance   police basic
creep fence   cent metric   clamp deceit

SUGGESTED PRACTICES
1. Underline c words you see in a paragraph. Write S over each c having its soft sound. Write H over each c having its hard sound.

2. Underline g words you see in a paragraph. Write S over those having the soft sound. Write H over those having the hard sound.

Additional Exercises

SINGLE CONSONANT SOUNDS: BEGINNING-MIDDLE-ENDING

A. Listen to the <u>beginning</u> sound of each word below. Think of a word that begins with the same sound. Write it in the blank that follows the word. If you are not sure how to spell the word, do the best you can.

Example: carrot *cake (or, kind)*

1. jagged_____ 2. ranger_____ 3. naked_____ 4. gravy_____

5. harem_____ 6. bandit_____ 7. book_____ 8. marry_____

9. dab_____ 10. zebra_____ 11. quick_____ 12. yes_____

13. liquid_____ 14. fried_____ 15. pig_____ 16. war_____

17. tell_____ 18. extra_____ 19. same_____ 20. value_____

21. card_____

B. Listen to the <u>middle</u> sound you hear in each word below. In the blank write a word that begins with the same middle sound you hear.

Example: valley *lake*

1. cabin_____ 2. facing_____ 3. modern_____ 4. duffle_____

5. wagon_____ 6. region_____ 7. behave_____ 8. injure_____

9. thinking_____ 10. salad_____ 11. humid_____ 12. manner_____

13. hyper_____ 14. equal_____ 15. stories_____ 16. inside_____

17. measles_____ 18. insure_____ 19. waiter_____ 20. severe_____

21. highway_____ 22. Mexico_____ 23. beyond_____ 24. razor_____

C. Listen to the <u>ending</u> consonant sound you hear in each word below. In the blank write a word that begins with the same sound you hear.

Example: put *take*

1. club_____ 2. stand_____ 3. thief_____ 4. wage_____

5. stag_____ 6. slick_____ 7. brittle_____ 8. dream_____

9. clean_____ 10. drop_____ 11. bar_____ 12. Paris_____

Additional Exercises

13. paint_____ 14. move_____ 15. nix_____ 16. checks_____

17. jazz_____ 18. oppose_____

CONSONANT DIGRAPHS

A. Each digraph below is followed by three words with blanks. Write the digraph in the blanks.

Example: ch as in chain *ch*_arge cat*ch*_er whi*ch*

1. ch as in chain: ____imney   ba____elor   pat____
2. ch as in choir: ____emical   psy____osis   a____e
3. ch as in chef: ____auvinistic   ____agrin   ____alet
4. gh as in laugh: tou____   rou____ly   trou____
5. ph as in photo: ____obia   as____alt   gra____ics
6. sh as in sheep: ____ave   bi____op   sailfi____
7. th as in this: ____ese   ra____er   wor____y
8. th as in think: ____ick   clo____   fai____
9. wh as in when: ____ite   ____ale   ____eel

B. In the words below underline the digraphs you see and hear; not every word contains a digraph. Circle the words that have no digraphs.

Example: chill   cough   (slip)   fish

1. champ 2. flake 3. smother 4. shave 5. private 6. chlorine 7. think

8. Philadelphia 9. this 10. Ralph 11. nephew 12. Chicago 13. method

14. laughter 15. whip

CONSONANT BLENDS

A. In each word below underline the, blend or blends, you see and hear.

Examples: drip   beast   friend

1. scrape 2. hand 3. place 4. blend 5. frame 6. scream 7. cream

8. brake 9. bark 10. clever 11. stripe 12. drink 13. shark 14. shelf

15. slave 16. gloves 17. Barbara 18. ski

Additional Exercises

B. Which blend makes a word in every given word? Write that blend in each blank.
Example: br or bl _bl_ aze _bl_ ister _bl_ under

1. bl or br	____acelet	____eeze	____idle
2. cl or dr	____awer	____ead	____ummer
3. cl or dr	____amp	____early	____over
4. dw or fl	____ight	____indle	____arfish
5. dw or fl	____avor	____ight	____oppy
6. fr or gl	____itter	____and	____ory
7. fr or gl	____ench	____ighten	____osty
8. gr or pl	____ace	____ip	____ound
9. gr or pl	____ain	____ot	____ump
10. sc or scr	____een	____immage	____utiny
11. sc or scr	____at	____ore	____otland
12. sk or sl	____eleton	____impy	____ylight
13. sk or sl	____ang	____iding	____oppy
14. sm or sn	____apper	____iffle	____ooze
15. sm or sn	____ash	____oky	____uggle
16. sp or spl	____are	____ecial	____ider
17. sp or spl	____atter	____inter	____otch
18. spr or sq	____uadron	____ueak	____uint
19. spr or sq	____ain	____ig	____out
20. st or str	____ab	____eeple	____omach
21. st or str	____ain	____ong	____uggle
22. sw or tr	____ail	____eat	____usting

Additional Exercises

23. sw or tr	____ab	____eater	____ish
24. tw or pr	____eezers	____itter	____enty
25. tw or pr	____ay	____ice	____ogram
26. rb or ld	He____	ga____	Ba____
27. rb or ld	Haro____	fo____er	shou____er
28. lf or rf	e____	gu____	she____
29. lf or rf	dwa____	tu____	wha____
30. lv or lm	e____	rea____	he____
31. lv or lm	revo____e	she____e	invo____e
32. lp or mps	sca____	pu____	whe____
33. lp or mps	cla____	stu____	chi____
34. mp or rk	fo____	la____	ma____ed
35. mp or rk	gra____	gru____y	ski____
36. rn or rt	mou____	ea____	adjou____
37. rn or rt	inve____	depo____	pa____ner
38. rl or rm	ala____	disa____	do____
39. rl or rm	Ea____	chu____ish	Ca____

CONSONANTS: SILENT

In the words below mark with a slash each consonant that is silent. If you are not sure how to pronounce a word, ask for help.

Example: wou/d /knee

1. psyche 2. ghetto 3. knuckles 4. glisten 5. doubt 6. gnu 7. honor 8. knight

9. numb 10. pneumatic 11. should 12. column 13. knock 14. bristles 15. sovereign

SUGGESTED PRACTICES

1. In a newspaper, magazine, or an assigned reading, circle twenty words in which you see a consonant blend or blends. Underline the blends.

2. In your readings, circle twenty words in which you see consonant digraphs. Underline the digraphs.

3. Repeat Unit Two Application Expercises on pages 31-32. Use different words.

UNIT THREE

LONG VOWEL SOUNDS

A. In the words below mark with the macron (−) each vowel having the long sound. Circle the words that do not have a long vowel sound.
   Example: wāit   tīme   (Tim)

1. seat   2. nest   3. ride   4. wall   5. awake   6. Bob   7. load   8. union

9. must   10. made   11. fly   12. habit   13. peeling   14. spoke   15. mule   16. bass

17. bind   18. gym   19. music   20. soak   21. body   22. still   23. ancient   24. pipe

B. Read the word on the left; listen to the long vowel sound. From the four words to the right underline the one having that same vowel sound.

	Example	ice:	silly	like	chain	bridge
1.	ice:	pill	pick		hit	mind
2.	feet:	spend	easy		let	great
3.	boat:	bomb	wrote		rob	got
4.	ate:	grand	pat		dance	blame
5.	use:	upper	union		stuck	house

C. Read each sentence below and the four words following the blank. Write in the blank the word having a long vowel sound.
   Example: The bus stopped at ___*Pine*___ Street. (Elm/Pine/Walnut/Apple)

1. At the end of the street is the _____. (office/jail/garage/lot)

2. The race is _____. (beginning/over/short/long)

3. They wanted to buy _____. (shrubs/flowers/sod/vines)

4. Ask the waiter for _____. (sugar/tea/milk/spoons)

Additional Exercises   119

5. The student asked for _____. (paper/pencils/chalk/scissors)

6. The letter was written with red _____. (ink/type/pencil/letters)

SHORT VOWEL SOUNDS

A. In the words below mark with a breve (˘) each vowel having the short sound. Circle the words that do not have a short vowel sound.

Example: thr˘ill   cl˘assy   (deep)

1. slip   2. gap   3. ice   4. unable   5. me   6. meant   7. fuel   8. help   9. shop

10. ask   11. throat   12. jetset   13. gone   14. thus   15. jade   16. hid   17. slope

18. chop   19. sent   20. shimmer   21. left   22. ant   23. feet   24. cave   25. fence

B. Read the word on the left. From the group of words on the right underline the word which has the same vowel sound.

	and:	late	car	rat
1. hit:	ice	find	drip	hijack
2. and:	face	map	pray	steak
3. shop:	bold	long	oil	not
4. nut:	use	cute	fudge	pound
5. lend:	we	great	leave	pet

C. In the blank in each sentence write the word having the short vowel sound.

Example: The bus stopped at __Elm__ Street. (Oak/Elm/Maple/Beech)

1. The first person to call was _____. (Kate/Mike/Jane/Kathy)

2. For breakfast the truck driver ordered _____. (juice/eggs/toast/grapefruit)

3. The clerk's name is _____. (Dale/Jim/Luke/Lyle)

4. The trainor tied the dog's leash to the _____. (gate/post/fence/stake)

5. Please buy the _____ for me. (wine/nuts/spoon/coat)

6. The people lined up outside the _____. (movie/gym/store/gate)

SHORT & LONG VOWEL SOUNDS

Read the word on the left. Listen to sound of the underlined vowel. From the group of words on the right underline the one having the same vowel sound.

          Example m<u>a</u>ke: sat   war   <u>able</u>   apple

1. c<u>u</u>t:	useful	sunny	beauty	suit
2. n<u>o</u>se:	sour	hop	slot	hold
3. h<u>a</u>t:	mate	pail	batch	air
4. f<u>i</u>t:	sick	file	pine	climb
5. <u>e</u>at:	bent	shell	send	cheek
6. h<u>o</u>p:	coat	clock	hope	one
7. h<u>a</u>te:	ham	ant	great	glad
8. b<u>e</u>t:	steak	edge	seen	jeans
9. f<u>i</u>ght:	wrist	fin	flit	ice
10. <u>u</u>se:	chunk	butter	flu	mutt

SCHWA VOWEL SOUNDS

A. In the words below mark with the upside down e the vowel having the schwa sound. Each word has one schwa vowel sound.

          Example: apr^əon   tot^əal   c^əontrol

1. ajar   2. condemn   3. parallel   4. collapse   5. rotten   6. expression

7. agree   8. fatigue   9. opium   10. spiral   11. equal   12. polka

B. On the blank in each sentence below write the word having the schwa sound.
          Example: He mailed the *helmet*. (swimsuit/baseball/helmet/T-shirt)

1. Did you hear the _____? (traffic/screaming/blowout/siren)

2. Watch for the _____. (starling/falcon/bluebird/sparrow)

3. Tonight they are going to the _____. (picnic/movie/ballgame/museum)

4. Buy the _____ ice cream. (blackberry/lemon/cherry/nutty)

5. Pick up the _____. (paintbrush/pencil/doormat/backpack

Additional Exercises

6. Adults and children hurried toward the _____.
(bookstore/circus/meetings/stairway)

C. In each word below mark with the upside down e the vowels having the schwa sound. Some words have more than one schwa sound.
Example: divorce   cannibal

1. palace   2. collection   3. lineman   4. syllable   5. economist   6. polka

7. division   8. reckon   9. policeman   10. ultra   11. political   12. virus

D. In the names of U.S. cities below put the schwa symbol over each vowel having the schwa sound. Some words have more than one.
Example: Atlanta

Los Angeles   Boston   Jacksonville   Portland   Dallas

Indianapolis   Houston   Savannah   Lincoln   Loma Linda

Plymouth   Richmond   Philadelphia

E. In the names of the U.S. states put the schwa symbol over each vowel having the schwa sound. Some states have more than one schwa sound.
Example: Arizona

Indiana   Texas   California   Oregon   Washington   Idaho   Minnesota

Illinois   Kansas   Tennessee   Alabama   Oklahoma   Massachusetts

F. Underline each word having a schwa vowel sound. Mark the schwa vowel with the schwa symbol. Not all the words have a schwa sound.
Example: cannon   mailman

1. magazine   2. mighty   3. stealthily   4. around   5. aging   6. cemetery   7. dampen

8. lonely   9. incident   10. waiting   11. afar   12. steamship   13. census   14. stealthy

15. dumpling   16. accent   17. economy   18. Johnson   19. gabby   20. buffalo

LONG, SHORT, SCHWA VOWEL SOUNDS
In the following words mark each vowel either long (−), short (∪), schwa (ə), or silent (/).
Example: victim   reading

1. felony   2. bucket   3. potato   4. sitting   5. Cuban   6. romantic   7. candy

8. statement   9. abide   10. fasten   11. vegetate   12. blindly   13. venom   14. bigamy

SUGGESTED PRACTICES
Repeat Unit Three Application Exercises 1 and 2 on pages 49-50. Use words from your assignments or other readings.

UNIT FOUR
VC, CVC PATTERN

A. Underline the words having the VC or CVC pattern and the short vowel sound:

Example: <u>hat</u> rate <u>if</u>

1. tap 2. cape 3. hand 4. hope 5. coat 6. Smith 7. able

8. ace 9. smile 10. flake 11. flap 12. jack 13. Jake 14. great 15. gap

B. Each sentence below has one blank. From the words following the sentence find the one having the VC or CVC pattern with the short vowel sound. Write that word in the blank.

Example: Did you buy a new fishing *rod*? (rod/reel/pole)

1. The waitress served our _____. (tea/muffins/rolls)

2. Carl ordered _____ for dinner. (beef/ham/snails)

3. We drove to the lake to _____. (dive/sail/swim)

4. Jim bought his wife a _____. (robe/ring/house)

5. We heard a girl _____. (scream/yell/cry)

C. In each blank following the vowel write a word having the VC or CVC pattern and the short vowel sound. The first word is given for you. If it is difficult for you to think of words, look for them in your reading.

1. a <u>jam</u> _____ _____ _____

2. e <u>pep</u> _____ _____ _____

3. i <u>will</u> _____ _____ _____

4. o <u>mop</u> _____ _____ _____

5. u <u>luck</u> _____ _____ _____

D. The words below are divided into syllables. Underline each syllable having the VC or CVC pattern. Mark with the breve (◡) the vowel having the short vowel sound.

Example: păn ic lăx

1. hap py 2. in struct 3. im peach 4. emp ty 5. odd ly
6. un til 7. ac ro bat 8. bone less 9. ex pose 10. gi gan tic

Additional Exercises 123

VC(e), CVC(e) PATTERN

A. Underline the words having the VC(e) or CVC(e) pattern.
              Example: _pose_   rat   _rate_
1. jail   2. ale   3. go   4. game   5. pace   6. pack   7. type   8. tip   9. pile   10. pill

B. Each sentence below has one blank. From the words following the sentence find the one having the VC(e) or CVC(e) pattern. Write that word in the blank.
    Example: Will you watch the Rose Bowl game with _Pete_? (Bob/Pete/Mary)
1. He reached out to _____ the horse's neck. (pet/stroke/touch)

2. Do you _____ for a million dollars? (hope/wish/play)

3. _____ the door. (close/shut/hold)

4. The pitch to _____ was high and outside. (Rick/Flo/Dale)

5. It's a _____! (hit/strike/fly)

6. Wear your _____ shirt to the party. (green/rose/red)

C. In each blank following the vowel write a word having the VC(e) or CVC(e) pattern. The first word is given for you. If it is difficult for you to think of words look for them in your reading.
1. a   late   _____   _____   _____

2. e   Zeke   _____   _____   _____

3. i   pile   _____   _____   _____

4. o   vote   _____   _____   _____

5. u   cute   _____   _____   _____

D. The words below are divided into syllables. Underline each syllable having the VC(e) or CVC(e) pattern. Mark the first vowel long (−) and the final e silent (/).
              Example: ūs/ ful   com pōs/
1. pro pose   2. re late   3. hope less   4. com bine   5. di late   6. fate ful

7. pre side   8. reg u late   9. ill u strate   10. de bone   11. rec og nize   12. ape man

124   Additional Exercises

CVVC PATTERN

A. Underline the words having the CVVC pattern. In the CVVC words mark the long vowel with the macron (−) and the silent vowel with the slash (/).

Example: ch*ī*ef b*ā*i̸l   bake

1. chain   2. cane   3. lake   4. fail   5. cold   6. coal   7. fried   8. cheat

9. mile   10. mail   11. claim   12. climb   13. sneak   14. snake   15. niece

B. Each sentence below has one blank. From the words following the sentence find the one having the CVVC pattern with one long vowel sound and one silent vowel. Write that word in the blank.

Example: The book is *cheap*. (thick/used/cheap)

1. After the crash the driver _____. (ran/cried/shook)

2. She wants to _____ math. (take/learn/teach)

3. Heavy _____ covered the shoreline. (fog/rain/clouds)

4. In which aisle can I find _____? (bread/soap/candy)

5. Please give the report to _____. (Gail/Mat/Clare)

6. Carol steered her trailbike into the _____. (woods/path/road)

C. Change the CVC pattern words below to CVVC words having one long vowel sound and one silent vowel. Write the CVVC word in the blank.

Example: red *reed*   pad *paid*

1. men _____   2. got _____   3. rod _____   4. best _____

5. clam _____   6. bran _____   7. pant _____   8. bed _____

9. wed _____   10. met _____   11. set _____   12. Mel _____

13. Jon _____   14. did _____   15. bled _____

D. The words below are divided into syllables. Each word has one syllable with the CVVC pattern. Underline that syllable. Then, inside that syllable use a macron (−) to mark the long vowels. Use a slash (/) to cross out the silent vowels.

Example: t*ō*a̸st ed   re pl*ī*e̸d

1. real ly   2. de rail   3. re ceive   4. croak ing   5. de crease   6. ap proach

7. re frain   8. boast ing   9. con ceit ed   10. be lief   11. main ly   12. be tween

Additional Exercises   125

CV PATTERN

A. Underline the words having the CV pattern and the long vowel sound.

Example: <u>she</u> kite <u>fly</u>

1. pro   2. prop   3. we   4. key   5. oats   6. ho   7. sky   8. scold   9. Flo   10. slope

B. The words below are divided into syllables. Underline the syllables having the CV pattern and mark with a macron (−) the vowel having its long sound.

Example: <u>cu</u> pid   whis <u>ky</u>   <u>fo</u> cus

1. re fuse   2. ha lo   3. stu pid   4. may be   5. le gal   6. de cline

7. like ly   8. stu dent   9. jum bo   10. cy cle   11. po ta to   12. Ro ver

C. Each sentence below has one blank. From the words following the sentence find the one having the CV pattern and the long vowel sound. Write the word in the blank. Words of more than one syllable are divided for you.

Example: The _rival_ team ran onto the floor. (oth er/ri val/home)

1. The hospital needs a _____. (heart/test/do nor)

2. Craig wanted to _____ the door. (close/try/lock)

3. The music student plays the _____. (cel lo/drum/trump et)

4. Before dinner the tourist found a _____. (lodge/mo tel/room)

5. He wears a trench coat so perhaps he is a _____. (news man/spy/mod el)

R-AFFECTED VOWELS

A. Look carefully at the following words. Every word has a vowel which is affected by the <u>r</u>. Find the r-affected vowel. Underline the vowel and the "r" that affects the vowel sound.

Example: l<u>ar</u>d   p<u>er</u>ky   m<u>or</u>tgage

1. plural   2. were   3. garb   4. short   5. flirt   6. fertile

7. germ   8. library   9. serve   10. bored   11. varnish   12. chirp

B. In each group of words underline the one word having an r-affected vowel.

Example: Grace   <u>Carl</u>   Rex

1. Chevrolet Ford Chrysler   2. regret praise failure

3. truck   car   train   4. rocket   orbit   project

5. crab   shrimp   escargot   6. immigrant   foreign   refugee

126   Additional Exercises

7. gracious   agreeable   warm-hearted   8. courtesy   respect   grace

9. rayon   burlap   brocade   10. birch   cypress   redwood

11. frankincense   myrrh   present   12. lubricate   grease   lard

13. wrinkle   furrow   crease   14. perch   roast   reside

15. hearth   screen   grade   16. rustic   rural   country

17. wicker   reed   rush   18. briefcase   haversack   trunk

19. string   fiber   thread   20. workshop   pray   sacrifice

C. Look for the vowels in the following words. Mark each vowel either long (−), short (⌣), r-affected (R), or silent (/).
Example: pärty ŭndeř wőrth

1. Norway   2. exert   3. there   4. curd   5. barter   6. Fortran   7. every

8. morning   9. forward   10. after   11. whisper   12. exercise   13. discord

14. surprise   15. tractor   16. partner   17. reward   18. marry   19. hardly   20. vapor

DIPHTHONGS OI-OY
Pronounce the words below. Underline each word that has the "oi - oy" sound you hear in oil and boy. If you do not know the word, try the "oi" sound. If it makes a familiar word then underline that word.
Example: coin   coincide   Royce

1. disappoint   2. poison   3. destroyer   4. avoid   5. voice   6. doing

7. Floyd   8. toilet   9. annoyed   10. decoy   11. joyful   12. going

DIPHTHONG OW
Pronounce each word. Underline each word that has the "ow" sound you hear in ow letters. If you do not know how to pronounce a word, try the "ow" sound. If it makes a familiar word than underline that word.
Example: prow   blow   owl

1. drown   2. snow   3. chowder   4. below   5. flower   6. knowledge   7. slow

8. how   9. throw   10. cow   11. drowsy   12. know   13. coward   14. scowl   15. trowel

Additional Exercises   127

DIPHTHONG OU

Pronounce each word and listen to the sound of the ou letters. If the sound is the same as in found underline the word.

Example: <u>sour</u>   couple   <u>hound</u>

1. proud 2. cousin 3. noun 4. couch 5. crouch 6. south 7. touch 8. boundary
9. our 10. precious 11. snout 12. poultry 13. pronounce 14. bout 15. washout

DIPHTHONGS OU-OW

Circle the words in which ou or ow sounds as in cow or found. Not every word will be marked.

Example: (stout) (chow) slow   youth

1. prowl 2. coupon 3. vows 4. pouch 5. fowl 6. jealous 7. crow 8. lounge

9. vowel 10. couch 11. slower 12. flower 13. mound 14. noun 15. rough

16. scrounge 17. tower 18. count 19. scowl 20. tour

DIPHTHONG Ô

A. From the words following the sentence, select the one having the ô sound. Write that word in the blank.

Example: The horse kicked her in the _jaw_. (arm/ankle/jaw)

1. He returned my _____. (balloon/salute/wallet)

2. She caught a _____. (salmon/ball/cold)

3. They flew to _____. (Austria/Alabama/New Jersey)

4. We cooked _____. (sausage/snails/fowl)

5. She does not use _____. (talcum/caution/soap)

6. He was in the _____ for two hours. (parking lot/laundromat/garage)

7. The prize went to _____. (Alice/Ralph/Paul)

8. Are you vacationing in _____? (August/January/October)

9. The memory _____ him. (angers/haunts/pleases)

10. Do you hear the _____? (laughter/squawking/galloping)

B. Underline the words having the ô sound. If you are not sure how a word is pronounced try the ô sound. If it makes a familiar word, underline it. Have your instructor check your completed work.

Example: <u>saw</u>   pal   <u>mall</u>

1. thaw   2. daughter   3. balance   4. dawn   5. cost   6. caution   7. wallet   8. haul

9. haughty   10. salmon   11. balky   12. applause   13. coaster   14. foster   15. vault

DIPHTHONG OO
Underline the words having the same sound as oo in <u>bloom</u>.

Example: shook   blood   <u>school</u>

1. snooze   2. cook   3. moose   4. stooge   5. good-bye   6. foot   7. booster

8. balloons   9. spook   10. door   11. Snoopy   12. crook   13. ooze   14. broad

15. woodpile   16. schooner   17. spook   18. brook   19. booth   20. blood

SUGGESTED PRACTICES
Repeat Unit Four Application Exercise 3, Pages 79-80. Use other words from your assigned readings.

SYLLABICATION

SUGGESTED PRACTICES

Find other words from your assigned readings and repeat Unit Four Application Exercises 4 and 5 on pages 86-87.

Additional Exercises

KEY
UNIT ONE

EXERCISE 2, Page 4

1. f u y n o d e 2. b j a u i w o 3. t a m e o c x
4. q i s r a y o 5. v h u g e i a 6. q b y e l a u

EXERCISE 3, Page 4

1. clear 2. edition 3. snow 4. crazy 5. gymnasium 6. handbook
7. feud 8. because 9. few 10. lively 11. charity 12. cowboy

EXERCISE 4, Page 5

1. h l n r v 2. i k p t x 3. c j m q r
4. e f l s z 5. d m p u y 6. g o p v x

EXERCISE 5, Page 5

1. clouds rain snow 2. ink marker pencil 3. hammer nail pliers
4. down next over under 5. famous king queen tyrant

EXERCISE 6, QUIZ

UNIT TWO

EXERCISE 7, Pages 11-12

1. (b)ook (b)eer   7. (l)ittle large   13. (t)wo table
2. (d)own (d)ark   8. (m)oney mean   14. (v)ote vest
3. (f)un fence   9. (n)ote ninth   15. (w)ide watch
4. (h)it hand   10. (p)ut pest   16. se(x) extra
5. (j)og jet   11. (q)uiz quick   17. (y)es yard
6. (k)ite kick   12. (r)oad ranch   18. (z)igzag zero

EXERCISE 8, Page 13

1. but about crib   10. picture upon help
2. dip today bread   11. quart acquaint -
3. first after half   12. red work for
4. hum ahead -   13. top little flight
5. jump injure -   14. very even leave
6. kind sunken drink   15. with always -
7. look believe all   16. x-ray text fix
8. man amaze from   17. you beyond -
9. not funny when   18. zero razor buzz

EXERCISE 9, Page 14

1. j (jockey) 2. p (parade) 3. N (Niagara) 4. b (behavior) 5. h (hurricane)
6. r (meter) 7. t (trot) 8. m (claim) 9. d (stupid) 10. v (concave)
11. l (mellow) 12. w (awake) 13. f (scuffle) 14. z (buzzard) 15. n (banner)

Key

EXERCISE 10, QUIZ

EXERCISE 11, Page 15
1. ̇certain (S) 2. ̇coat (H) 3. aṅcestor (S) 4. ȯccasional (H) 5. Pȧcific (S, H) 6. su̇cceed (HS)
7. ̇cigar (S) 8. voi̇ce (S) 9. vȯcal (H) 10. ̇coiṅcide (H, S) 11. Aṙctic (H, H) 12. ̇cyni̇cal (S, H)

EXERCISE 12, Pages 15-16   Answers will vary.

EXERCISE 13, Pages 17-18
1. ̇gȧg (H, H) 2. villȧge (S) 3. hu̇ge (S) 4. ̇grasslands (H) 5. messȧge (S) 6. ̇genealȯgy (S, S)
7. pi̇geon (S) 8. si̇gnature (H) 9. rėgard (H) 10. voyȧge (S) 11. ȧgree (H) 12. ̇genes (S) 13. u̇gly (H)
14. parȧgraph (H) 15. vėgetable (S)

EXERCISE 14, Page 19
1. lȯse (Z) 2. takės (S) 3. iṅsurance (SH) 4. teṅsion (SH) 5. puṙse (S) 6. lei̇sure (ZH)
7. ̇si̇steṙs (S S Z) 8. thou̇sanḋs (Z Z) 9. Texȧs (S) 10. ̇suppȯse (S Z) 11. intru̇sion (ZH) 12. commi̇ssion (SH)

EXERCISE 15, QUIZ

EXERCISE 16, Page 21
1. h (heaven)   2. z (zipper)   3. g (grey)   4. r (run)   5. c or s (the correct spelling is city)   6. f (frighten)   7. y (young)   8. q (quick)   9. b (bottle)   10. c or k (the correct spelling is <u>cover</u>)   11. j or g (the correct spelling is <u>juniper</u>)   12. s or c (the correct spelling is <u>same</u>)   13. w (win)   14. z or s (busy)   15. s (leisure)   16. v (flavor)   17. x or t (extra)   18. p (happy)   19. l (jello)   20. m (frame)   21. t (hurt)   22. k (like)   23. n (even)   24. d (hard)   25. g or j (the correct spelling is <u>fudge</u>)

EXERCISE 17, Pages 21-22

<u>ch</u>ase	ex<u>ch</u>ange	su<u>ch</u>
<u>ch</u>orus	hypo<u>ch</u>ondriac	tripty<u>ch</u>
<u>ch</u>ef	ma<u>ch</u>ine	musta<u>ch</u>e
-	lau<u>gh</u>ing	enou<u>gh</u>
<u>ph</u>ysical	tele<u>ph</u>one	Jose<u>ph</u>
<u>sh</u>ould	bru<u>sh</u>es	wa<u>sh</u>
<u>th</u>is	fa<u>th</u>er	la<u>th</u>e
<u>th</u>ink	an<u>th</u>em	fif<u>th</u>
<u>wh</u>at	a<u>wh</u>ile	-

EXERCISE 18, Page 23
1. <u>th</u>at   2. <u>sh</u>ip   3. <u>ch</u>op   4. rou<u>gh</u>   5. bo<u>th</u>   6. <u>ch</u>iffon   7. <u>ch</u>ur<u>ch</u>   8. <u>th</u>is
9. wi<u>th</u>   10. <u>ph</u>armacy   11. cou<u>gh</u>   12. wi<u>sh</u>   13. <u>wh</u>ale   14. <u>Ch</u>icago   15. <u>wh</u>i<u>ch</u>

EXERCISE 19, Page 23

1. (chocolate)	mustache	pinch
2. chaise	(champagne)	microfiche
3. chord	(architect)	headache
4. cough	roughly	(enough)
5. phonics	(dolphin)	digraph
6. shame	fishing	(ambush)
7. (them)	brother	breathe
8. thin	(method)	strength
9. whip	wheeze	(wham)

EXERCISE 20, Pages 24-26

bl   bl
br   br
cl   cl
cr   cr
1. blow   2. clean   3. crunch   4. brown
dr   dr
dw   dw
fl   fl
fr   fr
gl   gl
1. flower   2. frog   3. dwindle   4. drove   5. glow
gr   gr
pl   pl
sc   sc
scr   scr
1. play   2. scowl   3. grass   4. scrape
sk   sk
sl   sl
sm   sm
sn   sn
1. ski   2. sleeve   3. snore   4. smooth
sp   sp
spl   spl
spr   spr
sq   sq
st   st
1. split   2. squirrel   3. stage   4. Spanish   5. spread

Key

str str
sw   sw
tr   tr
tw   tw
1. twelve 2. sway 3. strange 4. travel

EXERCISE 21, Page 26-27
rb rb
ld ld
lf lf
rf rf
lv lv
1. weld 2. gulf 3. wharf 4. delve 5. garb
lm lm
lp lp
mp mp
rk rk
1. slurp 2. quirk 3. kelp 4. realm
rn rn
rt rt
rl rl
rm rm
1. start 2. storm 3. learn 4. unfurl

EXERCISE 22, Page 27
p̲rice	s̲neak	b̲lank	d̲rive	c̲lown	f̲rame
cha̲r̲t	s̲q̲uare	bar̲k̲	t̲wirl	s̲p̲leen	for̲m̲
b̲right	c̲reek	g̲low	sc̲o̲ld	shel̲f̲	p̲la̲s̲tic

EXERCISE 23, Page 28
deb̸t	doub̸t	comb̸
g̸nat	sig̸n	foreig̸n
h̸onest	h̸our	h̸onor
k̸not	k̸nife	k̸nowledge
cha̸lk	ta̸lk	wou̸ld
hym̸n	colum̸n	solem̸n
p̸neumonia	p̸salm	p̸sychology
wa̸tch	fas̸ten	mor̸tgage

EXERCISE 24, QUIZ

UNIT THREE

EXERCISE 25, Pages 35-36
ma̲ke ma̲in r a̲ ce   ne̲at she̲ r e̲al   ki̲te pi̲e l i̲ me
ro̲de bo̲at sc o̲ ld   mu̲le fu̲el u̲ nite

EXERCISE 26, Page 36

1. gō 2. whīte 3. rāin 4. māke 5. thōse 6. fīnd 7. cāme 8. cōld
9. pōke 10. līke 11. ūnion 12. grēase 13. plēase 14. rēmāin 15. kīnd
16. hūge 17. rēlāy 18. sterēō

EXERCISE 27, Page 36

1. m<u>e</u> 2. c<u>o</u>de 3. s<u>a</u>ne 4. s<u>o</u>ld 5. f<u>u</u>el 6. pr<u>e</u>view 7. m<u>u</u>le 8. p<u>a</u>in 9. gr<u>o</u>cery
10. s<u>i</u>ght 11. k<u>i</u>nd 12. r<u>e</u>m<u>a</u>in 13. m<u>e</u>an 14. p<u>a</u>per 15. pot<u>a</u>t<u>o</u> 16. subscr<u>i</u>be
17. evalu<u>a</u>te 18. st<u>a</u>tion

EXERCISE 28, QUIZ

EXERCISE 29, Page 37

h<u>a</u>t p<u>a</u>n m<u>a</u>n m<u>a</u>tch   b<u>e</u>t w<u>e</u>ll m<u>e</u>n r<u>e</u>nt   s<u>i</u>t <u>i</u>f <u>i</u>n p<u>i</u>ck
t<u>o</u>p j<u>o</u>b h<u>o</u>t f<u>o</u>nd   b<u>u</u>t m<u>u</u>ss s<u>u</u>n j<u>u</u>st

EXERCISE 30, Pages 37-38 Have your instructor check.

EXERCISE 31, Page 39

1. ĭn 2. păt 3. thŭmb 4. jŭmp 5. spŏt 6. ŭncle 7. wrĕck 8. skĭll
9. wăx 10. thĭnk 11. hĕll 12. bŭs 13. Smĭth 14. mătch 15. phlŏx

EXERCISE 32, Page 39

1. pet 2. under 3. humble 4. kitten 5. rat 6. sister 7. pocket 8. record
9. cut 10. getting 11. winter 12. stranded 13. sit 14. packet 15. reckless
16. success 17. pot 18. contract 19. racket 20. model

EXERCISE 33, QUIZ

EXERCISE 34, Page 40

1. băt 2. sĕnd 3. bōat 4. hūge 5. mŏp 6. cāve 7. lĭd 8. hōld 9. sēal
10. rōbe 11. tŭb 12. chīld 13. căn 14. pāle 15. ūse 16. lĕt 17. fĭn
18. lōad 19. nŏt 20. rēad 21. līne 22. fūse 23. hōpe 24. āpe

EXERCISE 35, Pages 40-41

1. hāte 2. clŏck 3. Jūne 4. ōats 5. pĕn 6. chăt 7. wīld 8. rŭb 9. clōse
10. rēal 11. fōld 12. kĭd 13. lōaf 14. pĭn 15. pĕt 16. cūte 17. māle 18. păn

EXERCISE 36, Page 41

1. hurrȳ 2. Nettȳ 3. cȳcle 4. babȳ 5. anȳ 6. mў̆th 7. dȳing 8. Sallȳ

9. prettȳ 10. sў̆stem 11. mȳ 12. sў̆mptom 13. studȳ 14. psȳche 15. dȳnamo

EXERCISE 37, Pages 42-45

sw<u>i</u>mm<u>i</u>ng _2_   v<u>i</u>br<u>a</u>te _2_   t<u>e</u>chnic<u>a</u>l _3_   vid<u>eo</u> _3_   sm<u>o</u>kest<u>a</u>ck _2_
k<u>e</u>r<u>o</u>s<u>e</u>ne _3_   d<u>e</u>f<u>e</u>ns<u>i</u>b<u>i</u>l<u>i</u>ty _6_   h<u>a</u>rm<u>o</u>nic<u>a</u> _4_   c<u>a</u>ref<u>u</u>ll<u>y</u> _3_

1. pat<u>e</u>nt 2. op<u>a</u>l 3. <u>o</u>ppose 4. d<u>i</u>vine 5. hopef<u>u</u>l
6. rap<u>i</u>d 7. chick<u>e</u>n 8. org<u>a</u>n 9. <u>u</u>nless 10. mel<u>o</u>n
11. summ<u>i</u>t 12. priv<u>a</u>te 13. parc<u>e</u>l 14. fragr<u>a</u>nt 15. <u>o</u>bject

EXERCISE 38, Pages 45-46

<u>Group One:</u>

brilli^əant   c^əanal   can^əopy   ^əerect   brok^əen   can^əary

cand^əle   ev^əasion   pris^əon   comm^əa   D^əuluth   famil^əy   app^əle

<u>Group Two:</u>

C^əan^əada   mat^əern^əity   c^əonvuls^əion   c^əonvent^əion   sc^əandal^əous

s^əubvers^əion   c^əonvert^əer   ^əopossum   intellig^əence   ap^əostle

<u>Group Three:</u>

s^əubmers^əib^əle   ^əAm^əer^əica   ^əauthor^əit^əar^əian   inst^əitut^əion^əalize

<u>Last word:</u>   s^əub^əord^əinat^əionism

EXERCISE 39, Page 46

1. ^əawāk^əen 2. sŭdd^əen 3. prĭs^əon 4. pūnȳ 5. sĕld^əom 6. frōz^əen 7. fĕl^əon 8. rĭ^əot

9. băll^əot 10. hās^əten 11. pŭnt^əed 12. lĕss^əon 13. ăt^əom 14. hămm^əock 15. hūm^əan

EXERCISE 40, QUIZ

UNIT FOUR

EXERCISE 41, Pages 53-54

1. dĭsh 2. stŏp 3. skŭnk 4. brănd 5. tĕnt
   cvcc   cvcc   ccvcc   ccvcc   cvcc

6. clŏt 7. scănt 8. drŭg 9. smăck 10. slĕd
   ccvc   ccvcc   ccvc   ccvcc   ccvc

11. drŏp 12. plănt 13. frĭsk 14. thŭmb 15. strĕtch
    ccvc   ccvcc   ccvcc   ccvcc   cccvcc

136   Key

EXERCISE 42, Page 54

1. lĭst 2. ădd 3. fĭlm 4. slŭsh 5. dŏck 6. bĕt 7. ĕgg 8. dĕnt

9. ĭmp 10. măt 11. bŏmb 12. snŏb 13. ĕnd 14. grŭnt 15. twĭn

EXERCISE 43, Page 55

1. mŭl ti ply 2. pro tĕst 3. Kĕn nĕth 4. ĭn văl ĭd 5. păn ĭc

6. ĕx ăct ly 7. ĭn vĕst 8. sŭp ply 9. ĕx pĕct 10. ĭn sŭlt
short

EXERCISE 44, QUIZ

EXERCISE 45, Pages 55-56

1. phonē / ccvce 2. ekē / vce 3. scrapē / ccvce 4. cubē / cvce 5. finē / cvce

6. fatē / cvce 7. shinē / ccvce 8. agē / vce 9. racē / cvce 10. stylē / ccvce

11. bonē / cvce 12. mulē / cvce 13. Utē / vce 14. thesē / ccvce 15. evē / vce

EXERCISE 46, Page 56

1. in flātē 2. dis trib ūtē 3. re cēdē 4. up grādē 5. hōpē ful

6. oc tānē 7. mis tākē 8. di vīdē 9. stātēs man 10. tīmē ly
long, silent

EXERCISE 47, Page 57
1. hate 2. fine 3. cape 4. note 5. shine 6. kite 7. robe 8. ride 9. rate 10. dime

EXERCISE 48, Page 57
1. ot 2. ote 3. iat 4. wan 5. giode 6. lite 7. ed 8. bude 9. vame 10. ub

EXERCISE 49, QUIZ

EXERCISE 50, Page 58

ea ee ei ey words:	mean heal bead read weed teen
	meet speak streak freak cheek sleek
	either leisure receive seize donkey kidney
ai and ay words:	bait pain main pay may say
	hay claim Spain spray tray

Key

oa oe ow words: oats moan coal Joan roast loaf
                  coach doe Joe foe hoe flow
                  slow blow

EXERCISE 51, Page 59
1. load ed   2. plead ing   3. treat ment   4. con tain er   5. ex claim

6. faint ed   7. roast er   8. pro ceed   9. be neath   10. re frain

11. ap pear   12. mean ing   13. clean est   14. Mc Clain   15. bloat ed

EXERCISE 52, Page 59
1. field   2. grieve   3. thief   4. shield   5. piece   6. siege   7. yield   8. diesel
9. believe   10. achieve   11. priest   12. wiener   13. niece   14. hygiene   15. chief

long, silent

EXERCISE 53, Page 60
1. shield   2. diesel   3. wiener   4. field   5. thief   6. chief   7. believe   8. grieve
9. piece   10. yield   11. achieve   12. priest   13. niece   14. siege   15. hygiene

long, silent

EXERCISE 54, QUIZ

EXERCISE 55, Page 61
1. so   2. Jel lo   3. lo cate   4. man go   5. ster e o   6. la dy   7. cu pid
8. flu   9. so lo   10. hap py
long

EXERCISE 56, QUIZ

EXERCISE 57, Page 62
1. peak   2. incline   3. had   4. grieve   5. lay   6. grain   7. goes   8. bland

9. strike   10. piece   11. soak   12. fuse   13. chief   14. freed   15. dis may   16. pray

17. smoke   18. boast   19. why   20. bus

EXERCISE 58, Pages 62-63   On Tape

EXERCISE 59, Page 64   On Tape

EXERCISE 60, Pages 64-65   To be checked by tutor or instructor

EXERCISE 61, Page 67

ch<u>an</u>ce	p<u>en</u>	st<u>il</u>t	sh<u>op</u>	n<u>ut</u>
ma<u>n</u>sion	susp<u>en</u>d	bu<u>il</u>t	fl<u>op</u>	sh<u>ut</u>
carav<u>an</u>	se<u>n</u>sible	k<u>il</u>t	st<u>op</u>page	b<u>ut</u>tress

EXERCISE 62, Page 67

1. filter 2. mention 3. standard 4. popover 5. scuttlebutt 6. stunned
7. banner 8. shunt 9. kilter 10. contentment 11. blunt 12. optional
13. Sanskrit 14. chopper 15. gunrunner 16. unbutton 17. filtration 18. nunnery

EXERCISE 63, Page 68

b<u>at</u>tery	c<u>at</u>alog	ch<u>at</u>ter	m<u>at</u>ter
b<u>at</u>ting	c<u>at</u>erpillar	Ch<u>at</u>tanooga	m<u>at</u>inee
b<u>at</u>tle	c<u>at</u>tle	Ch<u>at</u>ham	m<u>at</u>rimony

EXERCISE 64, Page 68

Answers will vary. Possible words: bad, cad, dad, fad, gad, had, lad, pad, sad, tad, brad, clad, shad, glad, haddock, bladder.
Check other words with your instructor.

EXERCISE 65, Page 69

1. b<u>atch</u> 2. h<u>atch</u>et 3. r<u>atch</u>et 4. c<u>atch</u>er 5. scr<u>atch</u>
6. s<u>atch</u>el 7. X 8. p<u>atch</u>y 9. X 10. th<u>atch</u> 11. p<u>atch</u>work 12. X
13. m<u>atch</u>maker 14. X 15. th<u>atch</u>ing

EXERCISE 66, Page 69-70

1. n<u>ight</u> 2. br<u>ight</u>en 3. dayl<u>ight</u> 4. del<u>ight</u> 5. fr<u>ight</u>ful
6. l<u>ight</u>ning 7. X 8. t<u>ight</u>er 9. ins<u>ight</u> 10. fl<u>ight</u> 11. br<u>ight</u>er 12. X 13. m<u>ight</u>y
14. X 15. r<u>ight</u>eous

EXERCISE 67, Page 70

1. g<u>old</u> 2. beh<u>old</u> 3. t<u>old</u> 4. s<u>old</u>ier 5. b<u>old</u>ness
6. billf<u>old</u> 7. uph<u>old</u> 8. X 9. sc<u>old</u> 10. b<u>old</u>est 11. X 12. c<u>old</u> 13. X 14. m<u>old</u>y 15. X

EXERCISE 68, Page 72

1. păt 2. pärt 3. phonĕ̸ 4. fōrm 5. cŭt 6. cūrĕ̸ 7. jär 8. jăm 9. vēry 10. rārĕ̸

11. pĕn 12. pĕr 13. cär 14. căn 15. nŭn 16. nŭrsĕ̸ 17. grōw 18. gŏt

19. cŭrvĕ̸ 20. hŭrrȳ

EXERCISE 69, QUIZ

EXERCISE 70, Page 74
1. broiler   2. decoy   3. poison   4. coin   5. avoid   6. join   7. uncoil   8. loyal
9. moisture   10. soy   11. oyster   12. typhoid   13. Roy   14. boyish   15. soil

EXERCISE 71, Page 74
1. (powwow)   2. blown   3. (bounce)   4. (shout)   5. could   6. (shower)   7. cough
8. (sprout)   9. (grouchy)   10. your   11. lawnmower   12. (blouse)   13. spacious
14. (couch)   15. (gown)

EXERCISE 72, QUIZ

EXERCISE 73, Page 75
1. audience   2. fraud   3. chalk   4. ballet   5. auto   6. cough   7. rough   8. waltz
9. auction   10. calf   11. lawn   12. auger   13. boss   14. awake   15. sauce
16. half   17. nautical   18. palace   19. alcohol   20. though

EXERCISE 74, QUIZ

EXERCISE 75, Page 76
1. boot   2. zoo   3. foot   4. brushwood   5. brooch   6. bridegroom   7. lookout
8. bloodshed   9. pool   10. noose   11. bamboo   12. redwood   13. cocoon
14. noonday   15. igloo

EXERCISE 76, QUIZ

EXERCISE 77, Pages 81-82
1. co zy   2. fe mur   3. lo tus   4. na tive   5. pro voke
6. An gels   7. Yan kees   8. Bron cos   9. Phil lies   10. Ben gals
11. Ti gers   12. par rot   13. do pa   14. Pad res   15. em ber
16. e mir   17. dor mer   18. em cee   19. hom burg   20. mur der

EXERCISE 78, Page 83
1. re - place   2. re - sur - face   3. un - even   4. un - hap - py   5. dis - fav - or
6. un - end - ing   7. dis - in - fect   8. mis - for - tune   9. dis - col - or
10. mis - lead   11. pre - ar - range   12. dir - ect   13. pre - can - cer - ous
14. re - in - force   15. pre - con - ceive

EXERCISE 79, Page 84
1. agree__ment__   2. act__or__   3. stubborn__ness__   4. import__ance__   5. art__ist__
6. broad__en__   7. energ__ize__   8. activ__ate__   9. glor__ify__
10. care__ful__   11. mold__y__   12. ignor__ant__   13. delici__ous__   14. child__ish__

EXERCISE 80, QUIZ

UNIT FIVE

EXERCISES 81, 82, 83, Pages 91-94 Answers will vary.

EXERCISE 84, Page 94
1. Christmas   2. carelessly   3. leather   4. angrily   5. stooped

EXERCISE 85, Page 95 Answers will vary.

EXERCISE 86, Pages 95-96
1. tired   2. gloomy   3. depressed   4. moody   5. private   6. trespassing
7. Beware of dog   8. Drive Slowly

EXERCISE 87, Page 96
1. shop   2. matches   3. frightened   4. boldly   5. filter

EXERCISES 88, 89, 90, Pages 97-100 Answers will vary.

EXERCISE 91, Page 101
   Winding through sub-arctic wilderness, crawling over a mountain pass, crossing icy creeks and a vague national border, the Chilkoot Trail was a part of Alaskan history. Miners in 1898 followed (it) from the slap-dash seacoast village of Dyea into the Yukon, packing a thousand pounds of supplies on their backs to get them through one year in the gold fields of the Klondike. They learned to hate all twenty-eight rugged miles of (it). Most of the miners walked (it) thirty-nine times in order to pack in all their supplies. Jack London himself trod (its) stones and waded (its) streams. The Northwest Mounted Police tried to keep law and order on (its) Canadian section, but they were dealing with the innocent, the desperate, the greedy, and the murderous. And most of these people were armed. For almost a solid year (it) was the scene of a stormy free-for-all. But by 1900 (it) was deserted and grass grew over the bootprints. The gold rush was over; the buildings of Dyea were knocked down and hauled off to Skagway. The Chilkoot trail was abandoned by people, and only the bears left their tracks in (its) dust.

EXERCISE 92, Pages 101-102
   The village of Talkeetna sits in the middle of Alaska. Perched on a railroad that runs between Fairbanks and Anchorage, nestled in between mountains and forest, and stuck at the end of a two-lane road, (it) seems to embody whatever Alaska stands for. Full of fiercely independent people who hold a moose-dropping festival every July, (it) contains one gas station, one road house, one leather works, one grocery store, one gold-and-antler trader, one dirt landing strip right smack in the middle of town, and one street. (It) does have two motels, but only one has numbers on the rooms; the other just has the doors painted in different colors. (It) has several bush pilots who make a living flying climbing parties up to Mt. McKinley and also buzzing tourists around snow-clad peaks scaring the daylights out of both the tourists and the mountain goats. (It) also has a few bars; (it) just wouldn't be Alaskan if there weren't a few bars.

Key

EXERCISE 93, Pages 102-103 No Key answers

EXERCISE 94, Pages 103-104
1. freedom 2. himself 3. Pennsylvania 4. help 5. climbed 6. three 7. nailed
8. container 9. railroad 10. baggage 11. apparently 12. labeled 13. rode
14. Philadelphia 15. taken 16. arrival 17. reached 18. friend
19. nailed 20. discovered

EXERCISE 95, Page 104
1. clothing 2. dacron 3. nylon 4. materials 5. clothing 6. woolen 7. corduroy
8. trousers 9. heavy 10. corduroy 11. buttons 12. leather 13. jackets 14. Swedish

EXERCISE 96, Page 105
1. kinds 2. campers 3. automobile 4. refreshments 5. protect 6. compartment
7. photographer's 8. Indian 9. cotton 10. balloon 11. material

EXERCISE 97, Pages 105-106
1. years 2. century 3. explorers 4. strange 5. picture 6. silent 7. adventurer
8. named 9. married 10. sixteen 11. Pacific 12. headhunters 13. Japanese
14. American 15. brought 16. including 17. Johnsons 18. canoes
19. orangutans 20. various 21. native 22. white 23. Africa 24. rhinoceroses
25. wildlife 26. jungle 27. cranked 28. guarded 29. Winchester 30. tall
31. heavy 32. charging 33. rhinoceros 34. attacking 35. climbed 36. safety
37. elephant 38. terrified 39. protection 40. snakebite 41. four 42. bathtub
43. overnight 44. covered 45. cream 46. hair 47. servant 48. dangerous
49. pneumonia 50. climbing 51. closest 52. fashioned 53. night 54. photo
55. herd 56. elephants

EXERCISE 98, QUIZ

BIBLIOGRAPHY

Albert, Elaine. How: A Handbook for Teaching Someone to Read. Kalamazoo, MI: Raspberry Hill, 1986.

Amlund, Jeanette; Kardash, Carol; Kulhavy, Raymond. "Repetitive Reading and Recall of Expository Text." Reading Research Quarterly, Winter 1986, pp. 49-58.

Ausubel, David P. Educational Psychology: A Cognitive View. New York: Holt, Rinehart, & Winston, 1968.

Cunningham, Patricia M. "When All Else Fails.........." The Reading Teacher 41, No.6 (Feb. 1988) 514-517.

Dechant, Emerald. Diagnosis and Remediation of Reading Disabilities. West Nyack, NY: Parker Publishing Co., 1968.

Dechant, Emerald. Improving the Teaching of Reading. Englewood Cliffs, NJ: Prentice-Hall, 1964.

Dechant, Emerald. Reading Improvement in the Secondary School. Englewood Cliffs, NJ: Prentice Hall, 1973.

Duffy, Gerald G. and Sherman, George B. How to Teach Reading Systematically. New York: Harper & Row Publishers, 1973.

Duffy, Gerald G. and Sherman, George B. Systematic Reading Instruction. New York: Harper & Row Publishers, 1972.

Eckwall, Eldon, E. Diagnosis and Remediation of the Disabled Readers. Boston, MA: Allyn and Bacon, 1976.

Gaskins, Robert W. "The Missing Ingredients: Time on Task, Direct Instruction, and Writing." The Reading Teacher 41, No. 8 (April 1988) 750-755.

Gleason, H. A., Jr. An Introduction to Descriptive Linguistics. New York: Holt, Rinehart, & Winston, 1961.

Maclean, Rod. "Two Paradoxes of Phonics." The Reading Teacher 41, No. 6 (Feb. 1988) 514-517.

Paulston, Christina Bratt and Bruder, Mary Newton. Teaching English as Second Language: Techniques and Procedures. Cambridge, Mass.: Winthrop Publishers, 1976.

Peters, Ellen E. & Levin, Joel R. "Effects of Mnemonic Imagery Strategy on Good and Poor Readers." <u>Reading Research Quarterly</u>; Spring 1986, pp. 179-191.

Sakiey, Elizabeth and Fry, Edward. <u>3000 Instant Words</u>. Highland Park, New Jersey: Dreir Educational Systems, 1979.

Salasoo, Aita. "Cognitive Processing in Oral and Silent Reading Comprehension." <u>Reading Research Quarterly</u>; Winter 1986, pp. 59-68.

Saville-Troike, Muriel. <u>Foundations for Teaching English as a Second Language</u>. Englewood Cliffs, NJ: Prentice-Hall, 1972.

Schell, Robert E. <u>Letters and Sounds</u>. Englewood Cliffs, NJ: Prentice-Hall, 1972.

Zintz, Miles V. <u>The Reading Process</u>. Dubuque, IA: Wm. C. Brown Co., 1970.